Bachman's Warbler

A Species in Peril

BACHMAN'S WARBLER

A Species in Peril

Paul B. Hamel

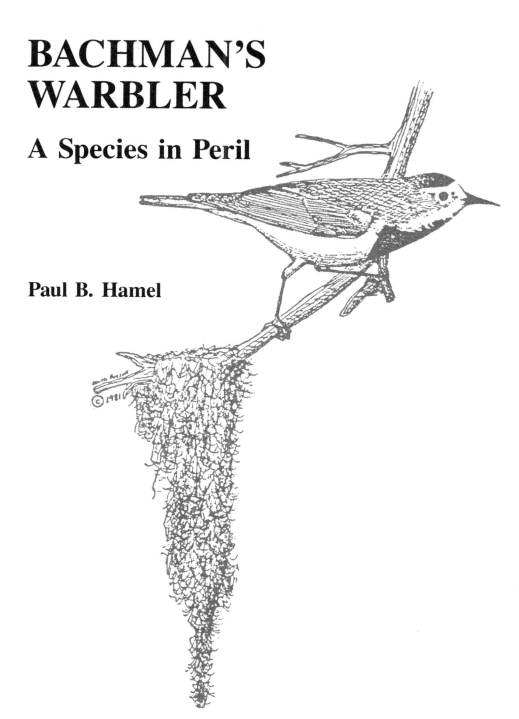

Smithsonian Institution Press   Washington, D.C.   London

Library of Congress Cataloging-in-Publication Data

Hamel, Paul B.
  Bachman's warbler, a species in peril.

  Bibliography: p.

  1. Bachman's warbler.   2. Bachman's warbler—
Bibliography.   I. Title.

QL696.P2438H36   1986   598.8'72   86-600113
ISBN 0-87474-545-4

54,534

Cover illustration © Keith Russell, 1981
Photographs on pp. 44 and 91 © Walter Dawn, 1978
Material from the M. C. Z. Wayne–Brewster letters used
  by permission of the Archives of the Museum of
  Comparative Zoology, Cambridge, Massachusetts

I dedicate this work to those
involved in the struggle to preserve
natural diversity.

Contents

Preface

This work was intended originally to be simply a bibliography in which all sources were presented and listed under appropriate subject headings; where disagreements or other circumstances necessitated, works were to be cross-referenced to each other. Recent reviewers have urged a more active authorship in which I evaluated the literature and identified important issues concerning the species. This I have done with some trepidation, but also with enthusiasm. Where my own researches have yielded new ideas or summaries, I present them as well.

The work comprises two Chapters, (1) an introductory discussion of the biology and history of the birds, and (2) a list of publications that mention the species. The first Chapter is a brief introduction to and analysis of the literature dealing with the biology and history of Bachman's Warbler. Certain works cited in the introduction do not mention the species. Such citations are marked by asterisks and the works are listed in a separate Literature Cited section that accompanies Chapter 1. Chapter 2 constitutes the bibliography of the species in which works are listed in two ways. First is an alphabetical listing, by author, of papers that treat the Bachman's Warbler. Second is a listing by subject categories. The subject classifications are patterned loosely after those employed in recent volumes of the Zoological Record. Subject classifications in Chapter 1 and the subject-heading section of Chapter 2 are labelled the same to enable ready comparison. I provided many categories so that works might be referenced as specifically as possible. Readers expecting each reference to contain a substantial amount of information must be patient, however; information about this very rare species is far more often recorded in phrases than in paragraphs.

Copies of unpublished reports listed in the bibliography have been placed in a file in the R. M. Cooper Library at Clemson University. Readers wishing to examine such works may do so by writing to the Reference Librarian, R. M. Cooper Library, Clemson University, Clemson, South Carolina 29631.

I have used a number of other important sources of unpublished reports or original fieldnotes in compiling this work. These include the field notes of Arthur T. Wayne at the Charleston, S.C., Museum; the extensive correspondence between Wayne and William Brewster in the collections of the Library of the Museum of Comparative Zoology at Harvard University; the correspondence of Witmer Stone at the Academy of Natural Sciences of Philadelphia; original field notes and correspondence of personnel of the U.S. Bureau of the Biological Survey in the Archives of the Smithsonian Institution; files of the Big Lake National Wildlife Refuge, Manila, Arkansas; files of the U.S. Fish and Wildlife Service Endangered Species Field Office in Asheville, North Carolina; and the files of the Wildlife, Fisheries, and Range staff unit of the U.S. Forest Service in Atlanta, Georgia.

Acknowledgments

I am indebted to many people for helping to bring this effort to fruition. Julian Harrison's preliminary bibliography was the starting point. Brooke Meanley and Paul Opler sent additional material. The following librarians were extremely generous with their time, insight, and energies in locating and verifying various of the publications: Donald Miles and Genevieve Reidy of the R. M. Cooper Library, Clemson University; Ruth Hill and Jane Baldwin of the Museum of Comparative Zoology Library, Harvard University; Janet Hinshaw of the Van Tyne Library, University of Michigan Museum of Zoology; Carolyn Hahn of the Smithsonian Institution Libraries; and Nancy Hackney and Sharon Bennett of the Library of the Charleston Museum, Charleston, South Carolina. I cannot thank these individuals and their institutions enough.

William Canine and Gordon Henry of Newberry College provided the photograph of the sculpture by Willard Hirsch. Walter Dawn graciously permitted use of his significant photographs of a singing male Bachman's Warbler. Keith Russell kindly permitted use of his drawing as the cover illustration. Sidney Gauthreaux and Michael Lennartz provided logistical support. Gertrude Corder typed difficult initial drafts of the manuscript. Gordon Howard, Pamela Purcell, and Maxine Romsa coordinated production of parts of the manuscript. Ruth Spiegel and Maureen Jacoby of Smithsonian Press have patiently guided me through the latter stages of the preparation of the manuscript.

The research for this bibliography was supported by the USDA Forest Service Southeastern Forest Experiment Station; the Clemson University Faculty Research Committee; the National Audubon Society; the Charleston, South Carolina, Natural History Society; and the Tennessee Department of Conservation.

An earlier draft of Chapter 2 (30 October 1978)
was read by James Bond, Eugene Eisenmann, Robert
Hooper, Thomas Imhof, Vernon Kleen, Kenneth Parkes, and
Henry Stevenson. As a result of their suggestions the
manuscript has been improved in numerous respects. Two
anonymous reviewers of a second draft of that chapter
urged the addition of a narrative account of the
species. Millicent Ficken, Orlando Garrido, Robert
Hooper, and Henry Stevenson read the draft narrative in
Chapter 1. Each made a significant contribution to
this final product.

In the end, of course, the work is mine, and I
take responsibility for all the analyses and particularly for the frequent speculations. I believe this
work is virtually complete, and regret any omissions I
have made.

Part 1. History and Biology of Bachman's Warbler

Interest in Bachman's Warbler (<u>Vermivora</u> <u>bachmanii</u>) has waxed and waned as populations of the species have seemed to appear and disappear over the 154 years since John Bachman collected the first specimen south of Charleston, South Carolina. Passage of the Endangered Species Act in 1973 by the U.S. Congress has sparked the most recent round of investigations of the species. No breeding populations are known, the spectre of possible extinction is unavoidably present, and a storm of controversy has developed over proper management of South Carolina lands where Wayne found a large number of nests in the early decades of this century.

Until breeding populations of the species are found, only the available literature, field notes, and correspondence can be used to guide the thinking of scientists, managers, and environmentalists alike concerning the conservation of the species. Bibliographies of previous literature were published by Sharpe (1885) and Ridgway (1902). No complete summary or synthesis of the literature has appeared since 1902, although Dingle (1963) and Stevenson (1972b) made strong contributions. Unfortunately much of the literature lies in old journals and works which are not easily accessible to most workers. Consequently, many recent popular treatments of the species suffer from inadequate summarization of known information about the birds.

This chapter is organized into sections and subsections after the <u>Zoological Record</u>. The same organization appears in the list of papers by subject heading in Chapter 2.

GENERAL

The greater majority of the General Works on this endangered species are not primary works but rather are

1

works that mention the species, or works that give a general overview of their author's knowledge of the species. Most of the sections in this category are self-explanatory. Field Guides and Illustrations are evaluated and compared by Hamel and Gauthreaux (1982). Biographies are those of individuals who worked on the birds, and whose biographers mentioned the species in the memorial account. In addition to the numerous illustrations, Bachman's Warbler has been the subject of a sculpture (Hirsch 1973) as well as the focal point for the social commentary of a popular comic strip (Trudeau 1981).

MORPHOLOGY

The morphology of Bachman's Warblers is described in the standard treatises of the late 19th and early 20th centuries (Baird 1858, Coues 1903, Ridgway 1902, Sharpe 1885). The original description by Audubon (1834), the account by Dingle (1963), and a recent summary of illustrations by Hamel and Gauthreaux (1982) serve as guides to the numerous descriptions of plumage.

More than 300 study skins of the birds are presently housed in North American museums (Table 1). The type specimen is held by the U.S. National Museum, as is the only known skeleton. Each of 300 specimens was examined, measured, and photographed under standard lighting conditions. Photographs of the specimens have been deposited in the VIREO collections at the Academy of Natural Sciences of Philadephia. Analyses of measurements of a sample of these skins indicated that sex differences in measurements exist among individuals in first basic plumage and among older birds as well (Table 2). Typically the male birds are larger. I attempted to use plumage variables to determine differences between birds collected on the breeding grounds along the Atlantic Coast and in the Mississippi Valley. No dependable differences were found so I do not present the tests. The results suggest that

Table 1. Specimens of Bachman's Warblers in United States and Canadian Museums.

Institution	Number of specimens
Academy of Natural Sciences of Philadelphia	13
American Museum of Natural History	80
California Academy of Sciences	18
Carnegie Museum	10
Charleston, S.C., Museum	15
Cornell University	5
Earlham College	1
Field Museum of Natural History	32
Louisiana State University Museum of Zoology	2
Massachusetts Audubon Society	1
Museum of Comparative Zoology	81
Museum of Vertebrate Zoology	8
Peabody Museum of Natural History	4
Reading, Pa., Public Museum and Art Gallery	2
Royal Ontario Museum	5
Tall Timbers Research Station	1
U.S. National Museum	39
University of California at Los Angeles	2
University of Georgia	3
University of Michigan Museum of Zoology	8
Virginia Polytechnic Institute and State Univ.	2
Total	332 specimens in 21 collections

Table 2. Comparison of external mensural differences of female and male Bachman's Warblers.

Measurement, in mm	Females		Males	
	Mean	S.D.	Mean	S.D.
	N=60		N=191	
Exposed culmen	11.5	0.59	11.7	0.62
Length of tail	40.7	1.62	42.3	2.12
Wing chord	57.4	1.45	60.2	1.67
Diagonal of tarsus	16.1	0.76	16.2	0.62
Length of white patch in outermost rectrix	10.6	3.41	15.0	7.4

Sample consists of potentially breeding birds taken N of 30 degrees north latitude. All differences significant at p=0.05. Sexes also differ in the shape of the patch of white in the outermost and second outermost rectrix. In each case the patch in males is larger than that in females.

Bachman's Warblers constitute a single monotypic species, as has been assumed by all earlier workers.

The birds have curved culmens that are distinct among _Vermivora_. They acquire full adult plumage only in the second prebasic molt, rather than the first (Hamel and Gauthreaux 1982). The single skeleton was part of the material used in a dissertation study on warbler morphology conducted by Shirley Ostroff (1985) that I have not seen. However, Jon Barlow (pers. comm.) indicated that the study revealed that Bachman's

Warbler was phenetically similar to Blue-winged (<u>V.</u> <u>pinus</u>) and Golden-winged Warblers (<u>V.</u> <u>chrysoptera</u>).

Bachman's Warbler eggs are well-described by Dingle (1963). They are usually pure white, although at least one with a few faint spots on the large end has been collected.

No Bachman's Warbler has ever been weighed, and none has ever been captured and banded.

EVOLUTION AND PHYLOGENY

Bachman's Warblers have been placed in <u>Vermivora</u> by all workers. Stein (1968a) presents a cladogram in which he associates the species most closely with Blue-winged and Golden-winged Warblers on characters of their vocalizations. I here suggest that the song of Bachman's Warbler may be additional evidence of relationship to those two species, on the following anecdotal grounds. In 1976, I conducted a song play-back experiment using Type-I songs of Blue-winged and Golden-winged Warblers (*Lanyon and Gill 1964; figured by Stein 1968a), Bachman's Warbler song, and songs of a "Brewster's" hybrid. The "Brewster's" song was similar to the Type-II songs of <u>V.</u> <u>chrysoptera</u> and <u>V.</u> <u>pinus</u> (*Lanyon and Gill 1964). Bachman's Warbler songs have never been distinguished into categories. Harry LeGrand assisted with the work, in which the songs were played in random sequence to territorial males. Allopatric Blue-winged and Golden-winged Warblers in southwestern North Carolina and southeastern Tennessee were the subjects of the tests. Our quantitative notes were lost when a tape-recorder malfunction occurred.

Two qualitative results of the work were (1) that the birds of both species responded to conspecific song most strongly and (2) that individuals of each species responded to Bachman's Warbler songs as strongly as to heterospecific Type-I Blue-winged or Golden-winged Warbler song. In several cases, both Blue-winged and

Golden-winged Warblers responded to Bachman's Warbler song with Type-II trill songs very much like Bachman's Warbler song. I therefore believe that Bachman's Warbler song is homologous with Type-II songs of the other two species. All three species appear to share the Type-II trill song figured for <u>V. bachmanii</u> by Stein (1968a, in his Figure 2); Blue-winged and Golden-winged Warblers have distinct additional Type-I songs. This similarity of Bachman's Warbler song to Type-II songs of Blue-winged and Golden-winged Warblers is further evidence of the relatedness of the three species noted above (Ostroff 1985). Unfortunately, the similarity is not such that it can confirm or refute the cladogram of Stein (1968a).

Bachman's Warbler may have been a hybrid, but the plumages are so consistent across the specimens I have examined that I believe that hybridization is an unlikely possibility for the origin of the species. Where and how the species evolved, whether it is an earlier or later derivation from <u>Vermivora</u> stock, whether Mengel's (1964) glaciation hypothesis is applicable to the species, and other questions about evolution and phylogeny remain unaddressed.

ECOLOGY

General

The single, most salient feature of knowledge of the ecology of these rare birds is the lack of hard, quantitative data. This lack of data dooms us to confusion, speculation, and often to controversy (see PROTECTION, below).

Understanding of the ecological role of Bachman's Warblers is hampered severely because no quantitative work has been published, because most of the qualitative work was done by individuals whose primary interest was documenting occurrence and not examining habitats, and because the great preponderance of work

on the species was done before knowledge of the role of
succession was widespread. Unfortunately, the birds
have become extaille (*Banks 1976) before detailed,
scientific work can be conducted on them.

Breeding Habitat

More than any other area of the ecology of the
species, breeding habitat has been the subject of
intense speculation and some analysis. Efforts
directed toward protection and management of the
species on the North American mainland have
concentrated on examination of the meager first-hand
accounts of nesting. These are Widmann (1897, 1898),
Wayne (1907a, 1910a, 1918, and his field notes at the
Charleston, S. C., Museum), Embody (1907), Holt (1919),
and Stevenson (1938). Hooper and Hamel (1977) and
Shuler (1976, 1977b) examined these data, none of which
are quantitative, and came to different conclusions
concerning what constitutes breeding habitat for the
species:

> "The overstory of areas chosen for
> nesting appeared to have been subjected to
> disturbance, either natural or man caused, that
> stimulated development of a relatively dense
> understory . . ." (Hooper and Hamel 1977);

> "To avoid the conclusion that these
> nests were found in the interior of a relatively
> mature, dense-canopied swamp forest one must
> assume Wayne was not describing what he saw."
> (Shuler 1977b).

Important habitat elements appear to be the
presence of trees for song perches and some foraging;
and dense understory thickets for foraging and nesting;
in a swamp, wetland, or area subject to periodic
flooding. Differences of opinion result from attempts
to identify the size and density of the canopy trees,
and the size of the understory thickets. Shuler

7

(1977b) echoed Wayne (Bassett 1941) that timber cutting
is disastrous for the birds, yet Widmann (1897) found
them in areas that had been selectively logged. Hamel
et al. (1977), on the other hand, suggested that the
birds may breed in secondary successional areas in
swamp forests. Remsen (1986) raises the interesting
hypothesis that the birds were specialists on cane
(<u>Arundinaria</u> <u>gigantea</u>). The photograph taken by Howell
(1911) is instructive in this regard (Figure 1) for it
shows both a relatively open canopy of large trees and
a dense understory thicket composed most obviously of
cane. Wayne's statements seem conflicting, for he
discusses the habitat as including piles of fallen logs
(Wayne 1901) and then indicates that cutting the swamp
caused the birds to leave (Bassett 1941). Likewise,
the field notes of A. H. Howell are confusing. He
observed [Missouri: St. Francis River (west of Senath),
April 25-30, 1909, notes in Smithsonian Institution
Archives] "Three specimens . . . and another one heard,
all in a brushy clearing in the drier part of the swamp
some two miles back from the river." Later he noted
(Arkansas: Big Creek, May 6-10, 1910, notes in
Smithsonian Institution Archives) "I located two males
. . . They were all seen in heavy primitive timber with
few openings and many dense cane thickets." These
notes and the comments of Wayne are open to more than
one interpretation.

A possible synthesis of the various opinions on
breeding habitat may be that the birds' original
habitats were secondary successional (i.e. gap-phase)
openings in the swamp forest canopy, such as might be

Figure 1. Breeding habitat of Bachman's and Swainson's
Warblers in northeastern Arkansas, 1910. Photograph
from Howell (1911).

caused by storms or insect damage.[1] All authors agree that the birds bred in swamps but no clear discussion has been made of where in a flooding regime the birds' optimum habitat occurred. Allen and Starr (*1982) suggest that differences in perception of the same data set may represent differences in the scale of examination. In my opinion, the scale of the disturbance is the issue here. We will never have a satisfactory explanation until breeding birds can be studied.

More quantitative observations have been made on single birds in a Virginia creekbottom (Barnes 1954, see Foraging and Feeding, below) and cutover woods of longleaf pine (Pinus palustris) in South Carolina (Chamberlain 1958). Neither of these birds was demonstrated to have bred, however; the one in South Carolina was in atypical habitat as well. Breeding was suspected of birds in a pond pine (Pinus serotina) pocosin on Fairlawn Plantation in South Carolina during 1948-1953 (Burton 1970).

Millicent Ficken (pers. comm.) suggests some general inferences that can be drawn from comparison with V. chrysoptera and V. pinus, the two supposed closest relatives of V. bachmanii. The former two are "'successional species' restricted to certain stages of

[1] For example, Williams (*1975) described such an area in the Hatchie River bottoms of Tennessee. Estimated to be 300 acres (120 ha) in extent, it was called in 1828 the "Big Hurricane." "'It is about a mile and a half--perhaps more--long, and about one-third as wide. . . . The Hurricane will best describe itself when you see it and go into it. I will say, however, that there is not an original tree in it. All were blown down or topped off by the tornado that passed over it; when, no one knows. From the appearance of the undergrowth, it must have been ages ago. Near the river it is thick cane; the middle and outer portion, every variety of scrubby undergrowth, filled up with briers. Except for the rotting out of the old fallen trees, or logs--many, however, are yet in a sound state of preservation--- egress into, or out of it, would be impossible.'"

old field or bog succession" that "probably shift
breeding areas frequently." They also "nest in
'colonies' where a number of pairs are often found if
the habitat is suitable." Bachman's Warblers may share
these traits with their congeners (see Breeding Habits,
below).

Territory

Widmann (1897) reported that one bird's territory
was 2 acres (0.8 ha). Barnes (1954) indicated an area
of 430 x 150 ft (1.5 acres, 0.6 ha). Two birds
reported by Chamberlain (1958) had territories "200-300
yards in extent" (8-18 acres, 3-7.5 ha) and 1.3 acres
(0.5 ha). These were apparently Type A territories of
Nice (*1941) although none of these estimates
distinguishes a defended area from an undefended home
range.

Migration

Bachman's Warblers were early migrants, leaving
Cuba in late February and returning as early as July.
Most of the movement through Florida took place in
March and August. Detailed observations of the birds
in the spring were made by Brewster (1891), Brewster
and Chapman (1891), and Wayne (1893, 1895). Atkins (in
Scott 1888b, 1890a) studied them on migration in the
fall. Birds struck the light at Sombrero Key in 1887
(Scott 1888b) and at Tybee Island, Georgia, in 1924
(Wayne 1925). No lighthouse or tower kills have been
reported since 1924. Jon Barlow (pers. comm.) has
suggested that the birds may be physiologically capable
only of short overwater migratory flights.

Winter Habitat

Unlike the case of breeding habitat, no detailed
descriptions of the winter habitats of the species have
been published. Most of the listed references discuss
limitations of winter habitat or restriction of the

11

birds' winter range. Amadon (1953) was the first to suggest that a restricted winter range was a possible cause of the species' rarity. Gochfeld (1979) points out that this is the only North American migrant warbler restricted in winter to Cuba. It is, of course, possible that the winter range extended to other islands in the Caribbean, such as Hispaniola, although no records have been made there. Terborgh (1974) and others assume that the birds' primary winter habitats were in the Cuban lowlands, especially in the extensive Zapata Swamp. Perhaps they were, but no quantitative surveys have ever been conducted. Qualitative observations, such as those of Gundlach (1876) and Garrido (1985) and the collections of Oscar Tollin for Charles Ramsden (specimens in the U.S. National Museum), indicate that the birds were found throughout the island from the western lowlands to the mountainous Oriente Province. They have been reported from native forest, planted forests, and gardens. Gundlach (1893) notes the birds as occurring in 'majaguales' (forests of <u>Hibiscus tiliaceus</u>) and states that cutting of the majaguales caused the birds to disappear. It is not certain whether this cutting was done for timber harvesting or as clearing for agriculture. Isolated winter records come from Okefenokee Swamp and from Melbourne, Florida (Dingle 1963).

Ecological Associates

Many writers, particularly among the early workers, mention lists of species that they encountered in the area in which they found Bachman's Warblers. Generally, the lists include species typical of the avifauna of bottomland hardwood and swamp forests. Except for the cases of direct interactions between species (see Competition, below), however, the lists do not indicate which species were actually syntopic with <u>Vermivora bachmanii</u>. Several nests found by Wayne (1907a, 1910a) were near those of Swainson's Warblers (<u>Limnothlypis swainsonii</u>), and he found nests of

Bachman's Warblers on the same day on which he first proved that Black-throated Green Warblers (_Dendroica virens_) nested in the Coastal Plain. Observations of both species were made in I'On Swamp. Garrido (1985) notes that the birds sometimes associated in winter with flocks of Yellow-headed Warblers (_Teretistris fernandinae_).

The species has never been recorded on a Breeding Bird Census, Breeding Bird Survey, or Christmas Bird Count.

Competition

Three authors mention interactions between Bachman's Warblers and other species. Atkins (in Scott 1890a), Barnes (1954), and Dawn (1958) note that the Bachman's Warblers were very aggressive toward other species, both on migration and on the breeding grounds. Barnes (1954) and Dawn (1958) each were dealing with a single individual.

Hamel (1981) discusses association in time or space and behavior between Bachman's Warblers and four other small, foliage-gleaning warblers, Orange-crowned Warblers (_Vermivora_ _celata_), Northern Parulas (_Parula_ _americana_), Black-throated Green Warblers, and Prairie Warblers (_Dendroica_ _discolor_), on the birds' breeding grounds in I'On Swamp in South Carolina. Orange-crowned Warblers, in particular, are nearly identical morphologically to the Bachman's Warbler by Hamel's (1981) measures of external morphology, and occur in coastal South Carolina nearly throughout the breeding season of Bachman's Warblers. He speculates that these species might have been brought into competition by ecological crunches of the sort described by Wiens (*1977).

Breeding Habits

Widmann (1897) presents the clearest available observations of the breeding habits of Bachman's Warblers and Wayne (1910a) also gives invaluable data. These observers, as well as Embody (1907) and Holt (1919), call attention to an unexplained aspect of the breeding of the birds. Each observer notes several pairs in close proximity. Observers at Fairlawn Plantation near I'On Swamp in the late 1940's also noted more than one pair of birds in a habitat patch (Burton 1970). Several speculative explanations for this trait involve the notions that breeding habitat for these birds appeared in limited patches, that patches might be occupied for a limited number of years, that a pair might occupy a patch and a small deme of its descendents continue to occupy that patch over the period of availability of the patch; other explanations are equally plausible.

The only certain knowledge of the breeding habits of these birds is that the males sang advertising songs from the trees in their territories and the nests were placed in shrubs. After Widmann, Wayne, Embody, Howell, and Holt, none has been privileged to study populations of breeding Bachman's Warblers. Stevenson (1938) found the nest of a single pair. Barnes (1954), Chamberlain (1958), and more recent workers were observing only single isolated individuals. No one has had the opportunity to examine Widmann's (1897) hypothesis that the older males acquired mates before the younger ones did. As far as known, the birds were monogamous; but even this statement reflects more the general case in wood warblers than specific fact about Vermivora bachmanii.

14

Clutch and Brood Size

Disagreement exists as to how many nests of Bachman's Warblers were discovered. Shuler (1979a) suggests 37 while Hamel (1977d) believes 40 is the correct number. The difference relates to interpretation of the field notes of Arthur Wayne. Shuler (1979a) interprets three entries in the notes as referring to three nests already discovered while Hamel (1977d) considers those entries to constitute distinct nests. The uncertainty is a result of Wayne's method of recording his notes. Shuler (1979a) gives a clutch size of 4.2 +/- 0.7 (range 3-5) eggs for 24 nests.

Timing of clutch initiation is a topic of some interest but one whose investigation requires rather a large number of assumptions. Length of time required for nest building, incubation, and raising young to fledging are unknown, as is the time taken between completion of the nest and laying of the first egg. Shuler (1979a) presents a projection of clutch initiation dates, and another is presented here (Figure 2). I have assumed that one egg is laid per day, incubation begins with the laying of the last egg and lasts 11 days, and that the nestling period lasts ten days. The assumptions are based upon the data in Bent (1963, see Dingle 1963). These projections for 29 nests indicate that the birds in South Carolina began clutches before 1 April in 18 cases and before 15 April in 26 cases. Three nests in Kentucky and Missouri were begun in the first two weeks of May. One of two Alabama nests was begun in the second week of April and the other about 20 May. These data suggest that the birds on the Atlantic Coast bred earlier, by perhaps a month, than those in the Mississippi Valley. Sufficient data exist in the notes of Wayne to compare timing of clutch initiation for four years, 1906 (four estimates), 1907 (seven estimates), 1908 (seven estimates), and 1915 (three estimates; Figure 2). The comparisons indicate that within a local population the

15

initial egg-laying periods in adjacent years may not
overlap.

No data exist to clarify the question of whether
the birds have a second clutch after successfully
raising a first brood.

Parental Care

Most nests of Bachman's Warblers discovered by
people were destroyed by their discoverer before the
eggs could hatch. Wayne (Brewster 1905) noted in one
case that the male parent was feeding the male
offspring and the female parent was feeding the female
fledgling; then he collected both of the young. Embody
(1907) discovered a nest by following the female, and
Stevenson (1938) noted that the male fed the young in
the nest. Thus, both adults were involved in the care
of the young, but quantitative data are lacking on the
relative contributions of the two parents.

POPULATION

Size

Populations of Bachman's Warblers in historical
times have probably never been large, but noticeable
differences between populations at one time and those
at another seem to have occurred. An overwhelming

Figure 2.   Clutch initiation dates of Bachman's
Warblers, inferred from the field notes of Arthur T.
Wayne. All data from I'On Swamp, South Carolina. A.
Date and condition when found, 35 nests; not shown is
nest found on 2 June 1906 from which young had fledged.
B. Estimated dates of initiation of 29 clutches. Bars
show estimates of date of initiation; numbers indicate
year after 1900, e.g. 13=1913. Only estimates accurate
to within four days are included. C. Estimated dates
of clutch initiation for all years for which at least
three estimates were available. Bars show contiguous
estimated periods of clutch initiation, numbers
indicate number of clutches initiated during the
period.

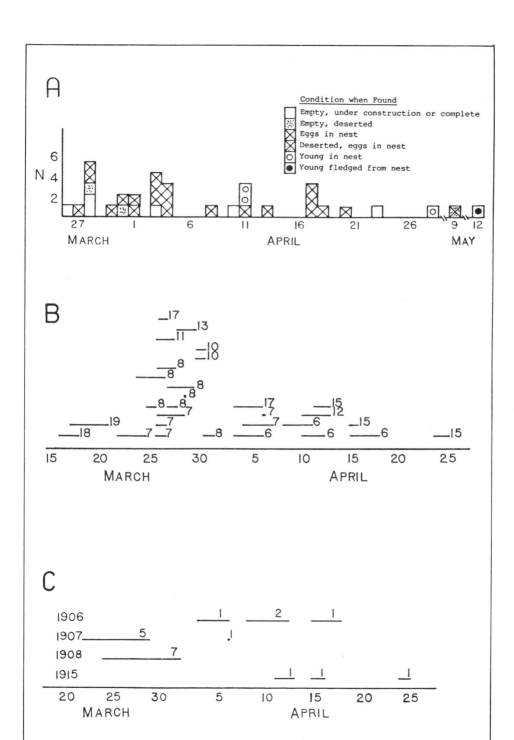

number of accounts of the species point out that, after the discovery of the birds in 1832 and 1833, more than 50 years passed before any were found again in the United States. "Rediscovery" is a popular word in this context. Gundlach (1855) had, of course, observed them in Cuba in the interim. After Galbraith's (1886) collections showed that the birds were present, collectors and scientists found the birds in some numbers during 1890-1920. Subsequent to that time the populations have been very low. At the present time no breeding populations are known, and the species has been described as "essentially extinct" on Cuba (Garrido 1985).

This historical record falls into three periods, pre-1890, 1890-1930, and post-1930. Interpretation of the record is essentially speculation, but I believe interpretation may shed some light on the status of the species and its decline. Two assumptions about the record are as follows: (1) that the historical record of observations reflects actual populations of the birds, and (2) that the record reflects ornithological interest and opportunity to observe the birds. These assumptions are not mutually exclusive but they do represent the endpoints of a spectrum of possible interpretations of the historical record of the Bachman's Warbler.

Under assumption (1), Bachman's Warbler numbers have gone through a cycle in the past 150 years, from low in the time of their discovery to high at the turn of the century, to lower in the 1930's-1950's, to extremely few now. Explanation of such a cycle requires a controlling factor capable of causing population increases or reductions. Periodic Cuban hurricanes are one such factor, disease is another, failure of food supplies either on the breeding or the winter grounds is a fourth, catastrophe during migration is another still.

Only one of these factors can be examined in any detail, the frequency of Cuban hurricanes. Absence of such storms indicates a possibly favorable wintering environment. Presence of such storms only indicates the possibility that large-scale losses of wintering Bachman's Warblers occurred. Fluctuations in the frequency of intense storms would then lead to population fluctuations in Bachman's Warblers, other things being equal. The record of storms for the 19th century is not as good as that for the 20th, but it becomes increasingly good in the latter part of the 19th century. Tannehill (*1945) reports that the most destructive Cuban storms are usually late season storms in October or November. Four such storms were recorded in the 19th century, in 1812, 1844, 1846, and 1865 (Table 3). Those in 1844 and 1846 were particularly strong. Thirteen such storms crossed Cuba in the first 44 years of the 20th century, and five of them occurred between November 1932 and October 1935. Two such storms struck western Cuba in October 1933; that in November 1932 is considered one of the most destructive and intense ever recorded (*Tannehill 1945). These storms may have destroyed large numbers of Bachman's Warblers as they did of other species (*Huntington and Barbour 1936). Cry (*1965) presents another view of the record of hurricanes that is not entirely in accord with that of Tannehill (*1945). Whether severe hurricanes actually caused significant mortality of Bachman's Warblers is unknowable; they did lead Griscom (1948) to suggest first that hurricanes may have been a factor in the decline of the species.

Under assumption (2), the lack of records of the birds between the 1830's and 1880's reflects only the lack of opportunity for collectors to encounter the birds. However, no evidence exists that collectors' interest in the birds changed between this and the later period. Population sizes in the interim are unknown but they were potentially as high as when the

Table 3. Cuban hurricanes of the 19th and early 20th centuries, from Tannehill (*1945).

| Era | Month | | | | | |
	June	July	Aug	Sept	Oct	Nov
19th century						
Total storms[1]	1	0	6	3	4	0
1900-1945						
Strong storms	3	1	1	7	9	4
Weaker storms	2	0	2	4	7	5
Total storms	5	1	3	11	16	9

[1]Two additional storms were reported but the time was not indicated for them.

birds were studied during 1890-1920. This assumption and the other do not differ in the projection of population sizes subsequent to 1920. Under this assumption the destructive hurricanes of the 1930's appear as a serious blow to populations already reduced to low numbers by some other cause. Indeed, under this assumption no natural cause of the decline of the species is a likely one.

Endangeredness

Bachman's Warblers are considered to be nearing extinction by biologists who have worked on them in the breeding season (Stevenson 1982) and in the winter (Garrido 1985). No individuals have been found on territory since 1962 or 1963 (Shuler 1977d). A female reported in Cuba in 1981 (Ripley and Moreno 1981) was the first bird observed on that island in 15 years.

Numerous suggestions, theories, and speculations have been put forward to explain the decline of the species. Each has focused upon a particular concern of its author, but no comprehensive attempt to relate the theories to each other has been made. The commonly cited reasons for the decline of Bachman's Warblers are as follows: habitat destruction, both on the winter (Terborgh 1974, Rappole et al. 1983) and breeding grounds (Korte and Fredrickson 1977, Shuler 1977b, Remsen 1986, many others); restricted winter range (Amadon 1953); overcollecting (Wright 1976); and hurricanes (Griscom 1948). Henry Stevenson (pers. comm.) considers none of these to be a very satisfactory or plausible explanation of the decline of the species. Millicent Ficken (pers. comm.) suggests that ecological specializations, indicated by their sharp bills and apparently narrow habitat requirements, made these birds "especially vulnerable if specific habitats were destroyed."

Any explanation of the decline of the species must also include discussion of the pre-Columbian habitat and range of the species, the geologic history of the birds' range, climatic change and weather, the possible roles of interactions with other species, failure of food resources, disease, and the interaction of these factors. No comprehensive data exist concerning the validity of any inference, however. A chronicler of these birds can do nothing more than arrange a mutually consistent set of speculations. I present these speculations to stimulate readers to think in ways that may enable action to prevent other species from needlessly reaching the perilous condition of the Bachman's Warblers at the time of this writing.

Prior to colonization of the Western Hemisphere by European and African peoples, Bachman's Warblers migrated to and from winter grounds somewhere in Cuba or nearby islands to breed in the southeastern United States. Breeding habitats that met the descriptions of

Widmann (1897), Wayne (1907a), Howell (notes in U.S. National Museum), and Holt (1919) were present at those times, and were produced in a frequency capable of supporting populations of the species. Winter habitats also existed in sufficient quantity to support the species. Possible agents involved in the production of breeding habitats were thunderstorms and tornados, hurricanes, fire, natural mortality of trees, and possibly the actions of native American peoples. Each of these factors is capable of producing disturbance to the forest canopy such that a mosaic of small openings is created in swamp forest. Under such openings would flourish the canebrakes proposed as important to the birds by Remsen (1986). Although winter habitat requirements are unknown, similar forces are likely to have produced them.

One factor not yet associated with Bachman's Warbler decline is the decrease in gross area of winter habitat at the end of Pleistocene glaciation. At the peak of the last glaciation, sea levels in the Atlantic Ocean were as much as 100 m lower than they are now (*Flint 1957). At that time the total area of potential winter habitat in western Cuba was much greater than it is today, particularly in the region of the great Zapata Swamp thought to be an important winter habitat by many (cf. Terborgh 1974, Ripley and Moreno 1981). The Isle of Pines may even have been connected to the main island. Simultaneously and even more strikingly, the extent of the Bahama Islands was severalfold greater than it is at present. At the time of glacial retreat the extent of each of these areas began to recede, as did those of other as yet undiscovered wintering sites. A first reason for the decline of the birds' numbers is thus probably the restriction of winter habitat (Amadon 1953).

Whatever the evolutionary reason for the restriction of Bachman's Warblers to a small winter range, other associated and unknown circumstances

caused the birds to migrate north early in the spring
and to return south early in the fall as well. The
early spring migration meant that the birds moved at a
time when favorable southeast winds generally prevailed
in the northern part of the Caribbean (*Bradley 1972).
Fall migration in August occurred just before and
during hurricane season.

The causes for the timing of these movements are
unknown, but some of the potential effects of weather
on populations of the birds are obvious. Adverse
weather on migration has caused innumerable groundings
of migrants; tower and lighthouse kills are known even
among Bachman's Warblers (Bassett 1941, Atkins in Scott
1888b). Adverse weather in winter may have been an
even more serious threat. Tannehill (*1945) reports
that the most serious hurricanes that hit Cuba do so in
October and November; the entire Bachman's Warbler
population is on the island at that time. Devastating
hurricanes may well have decimated populations of the
birds periodically. Huntington and Barbour (*1936)
describe the effects of one particular storm that
virtually eliminated bird populations in one part of
Cuba for a time.

We must assume that Bachman's Warbler populations
had experienced the effects of shrinking winter range,
periodic creation of breeding habitat, and periodic
severe storms on the winter grounds before colonization
of the Western Hemisphere. It is uncertain whether the
birds' populations were in equilibrium with these
factors, or whether populations were declining from the
action of these factors.

Possible insight into the situation may come from
landscape-scale considerations. For example, Shugart
(*1984) examines the equilibrium of vegetated landscape
systems as an interaction of land area with extent and
frequency of disturbance. He suggests that perhaps
only Cuba among Caribbean islands may be able to
support a landscape in equilibrium despite hurricane

23

disturbance. An equilibrium landscape on Cuba would be expected to provide a relatively constant supply of winter habitat for Bachman's Warblers at the present time. Other, smaller islands would not. In previous times of greater land extent, particularly in the Bahamas, equilibrium conditions may have existed such that Bachman's Warbler winter habitat was dependably present in other islands as well as Cuba.

After colonization of Cuba and the southeastern part of the United States, permanent habitat destruction became a factor both on the breeding grounds and in the winter range. Korte and Fredrickson (1977) graphically portray the destruction of bottomland forests in the Mississippi Valley using Missouri as an example. Kochtitsky (*1957) gives a firsthand account of the motivation of those who eradicated these forests. Terborgh (1974) and Rappole et al. (1983) both point out the clearing of large areas of lowlands in Cuba for sugarcane production. This clearing may have created disequilibrium vegetation conditions on the Cuban wintering grounds. Habitat destruction on breeding and winter grounds probably had a depressing effect on Bachman's Warbler populations.

The nature of human intervention into the birds' habitats requires additional discussion, particularly on the breeding grounds. Bachman's Warbler populations persisted in I'On Swamp in South Carolina alongside agricultural interests (Urbston et al. 1979), and in spite of some logging. Wayne (Bassett 1941) believed that logging in the swamp was what finally extirpated the birds from I'On Swamp (see below for an alternate speculation). Most perplexing in this regard are the populations in southern Missouri and northeastern Arkansas. From the time Widmann (1896, 1897) discovered the birds breeding there until the time Howell (1911, Figure 1) studied the birds, the bottomlands of the Mississippi River were undergoing

high-grade logging in which only merchantable timber
was cut. The birds reached their greatest local
population densities during these times, densities
great enough that Widmann (1907) and Howell (1911) both
labelled the species as "common". I believe that the
logging served to create the moderate disturbance to
the forest canopy under which Bachman's Warblers could
flourish. Proof of these assertions can probably never
be mustered. Some considerable circumstantial evidence
is available. In 1887 a logging tram railroad was
begun which ran east from Paragould, Arkansas, toward
the St. Francis River (*Horner 1973). The purpose for
building the railroad was the removal of timber to
sawmills in Paragould. By 1895 the line had been
extended to Cardwell, Missouri. In the early 1890's a
sawmill was constructed 10 mi (16 km) down that tram by
Mr. A. R. Byrd on Buffalo Island in Dunklin County,
Missouri. In 1896 Widmann rode that train and
discovered Bachman's Warblers in Greene County,
Arkansas. A year later he rode the train to Buffalo
Island (also called Kolb or Culp Island) and found the
first nest of the species in a clearing created by the
logging. Today, Arbyrd, Missouri stands on the site of
Mr. Byrd's sawmill. Further circumstantial indication
of the appearance of Bachman's Warbler habitat in those
areas is available in the form of the photograph by
Howell (1911; Figure 1) of both Bachman's and
Swainson's Warbler habitats. Had the birds been as
common in those areas in earlier times we should have
some record of them, but none exists. I believe that
the initial high-grade logging practices created
Bachman's Warbler habitats in bottomland forests.

The nature of the disruption of the original
bottomland forests in Missouri and Arkansas changed as
the emphasis changed from logging to clearing and
planting. Formation of drainage districts,
construction of levees, and channelization of streams
followed the initial logging with incredible rapidity
(*Nolen 1913). By 1920 much of what had been

apparently ideal breeding habitat had been completely cleared and drained for agricultural purposes. It was at this time that habitat destruction became a possible factor in the decline of the species.

Wright (1976) and some others suggest that scientific and economic collecting may have been an important factor in the decline of Bachman's Warblers. My own speculation is that collecting was probably not an important factor in the range-wide decline of the species. However, in selected local areas, particularly in I'On Swamp in South Carolina, local populations may have been adversely affected by collectors. Wayne (letter to Brewster, 4 June 1912, in collections of Library of Museum of Comparative Zoology) assumed that these birds would renest after a clutch was collected. His notes and the dates of collections reflect this belief, but he left no notes to indicate that he returned to the swamp to verify his assumption. The pattern of collections in his notes (Table 4) is consistent with the view that his persistent collecting reduced the population to a low level; 21 nests with eggs or young were taken in I'On Swamp, in 1906-1908, but he found no more than three nests in any subsequent year. This pattern is, unfortunately, also consistent with the view that the habitat changed through succession to a stage unfavorable to these birds, and consistent as well with a view that the market for clutches of eggs became flooded and the reduced price made other specimens more valuable. This third view is perhaps less likely than the others because of the high value ($75-200) that individual egg sets brought to Wayne (Shuler 1977d; Wayne letter to Brewster, 10 September 1911, in collections of Library of Museum of Comparative Zoology).

A summary of the forces involved in the decline of Bachman's Warblers, as I see them, is as follows. In times of glacial advance during the Pleistocene the birds had a significantly larger winter range on Cuba and the Bahamas, and perhaps elsewhere in the Caribbean as well. Population levels were in equilibrium with environmental factors that created habitats and caused mortality on migration and winter grounds. Under certain circumstances of unfavorable conditions the birds may have experienced ecological crunches during which they may have competed for resources with other species.

Table 4. Nests of Bachman's Warblers found and presumably collected by Arthur T. Wayne in I'On Swamp, Charleston County, South Carolina.

Year	1905 . . . .1910 . . . . 1915 1920												
Number of nests	1	6	6	9	0	3	1	1	1	0	3	1 2 1 1	0

Data taken from notes of A. T. Wayne in Charleston, S. C., Museum as summarized by Hamel (1977d).

In post-glacial times the winter range of Bachman's Warblers shrank with increases in sea levels. The reduced winter range may have increased the amplitude of population fluctuations resulting from winter mortality that was due to hurricanes. This alone may have been the single most important ultimate cause of the decline in the numbers of these birds. Colonization of both winter and breeding habitats by non-native peoples set in motion a sequence of events by which habitat availability monotonically decreased. Current evidence suggests that not only the amount of habitat but also its quality decreased, viz-a-viz loss of canebrakes or some other unknown requirements (Remsen 1986). Holder (*1970) points out that canebrakes were the first target for land clearing

activities because they grew on fertile soil and the
absence of trees made the canebrakes easy to clear.
These habitat losses apparently widened the amplitude
of population fluctuations such that a major
catastrophic mortality event, such as that suspected
from the Cuban hurricanes of the early 1930's, may have
eliminated most of the population. Populations are so
small today that individuals may be unable to find each
other on the breeding grounds, that normal nest
predation may be disastrous, that inbreeding may
interfere with reproductive success, that Brown-headed
Cowbird (Molothrus ater) parasitism may be significant,
or that other, stochastic processes may have potentially serious consequences.

Protection

Legal protection is afforded Bachman's Warblers by
the various Migratory Bird Treaties; by the Endangered
Species Act of 1973, as amended; and by the endangered
species laws of the states within the birds' historic
range in North America. Much of the recent history of
attempts at protection of the birds and their habitats
is unpublished and largely unknown.

Beginning as early as 1975, disagreement developed
concerning whether applicable endangered species
statutes were being followed in South Carolina on the
Francis Marion National Forest. The Santee
Preservation Society of McClellanville, South Carolina,
questioned the land management practices conducted by
the U.S. Forest Service in the I'On Swamp area of the
Francis Marion. Controversy over the difference
between the Society and the Forest Service led to the
formation of a blue-ribbon panel in 1976 at the urging
of Robert Golten, an attorney for the National Wildlife
Federation. Composed of the late Fred Evenden of the
Wildlife Society, David Marshall of the U.S. Fish and
Wildlife Service, and William Zeedyk of the U.S. Forest
Service, the panel met to discuss issues pertaining to
the protection and management of Bachman's Warblers and

their habitats. In March 1977, the panel convened a hearing on the species at Charleston, South Carolina.

As a result of their deliberations and the hearing, the panel tendered a series of reports (Evenden et al. 1976a, 1976b, 1977) in which they evaluated available literature concerning the land-use history of I'On Swamp (Urbston et al. 1979, Shuler 1976) and the biology of the Bachman's Warblers. Their final report included recommendations for Bachman's Warbler preserves in I'On Swamp and in nearby areas in the Little Wambaw Swamp and Wambaw Swamp, and for instigation of carefully controlled habitat manipulations to create breeding habitat conditions similar to those described by Wayne (1907a), Widmann (1897), Hooper and Hamel (1977), and others as discussed above.

Subsequent to the final report of the panel, the Forest Service entered into consultation with the Fish and Wildlife Service under Section 7 of the Endangered Species Act. The initial opinion rendered by the Fish and Wildlife Service (Vaughn 1978) was that Forest Service management was likely to jeopardize the continued existence of Bachman's Warblers on the Francis Marion. Based in part on findings of Urbston et al. (1979), and particularly the negative results of the searches for the birds on the Francis Marion (Hamel et al. 1976; Hamel and Hooper 1979a, 1979b), the Forest Service petitioned the Fish and Wildlife Service to reinitiate consultation over management of the Francis Marion National Forest. The final opinion rendered by the Fish and Wildlife in 1979 (Black 1979) is still in effect. Pending certain management activities to be conducted by the Forest Service, the opinion is one of non-jeopardy. The opinion includes recommendations for Bachman's Warbler management areas, for a series of experimental cuttings in specified areas of the National Forest, for annual monitoring for the species' presence, for a five-year review process, and for a system to encourage searches by the bird-watching community.

In 1982 and 1983, the Forest Service contracted initial bird surveys (*Forsythe and Tyler 1982) and instituted experimental cuttings in the recommended area. At about the same time, two of the areas suggested originally as Bachman's Warbler management areas, Wambaw Swamp and Little Wambaw Swamp, were declared wilderness areas by act of the U.S. Congress. No specific monitoring program for the birds was subsequently established and a number of the recommended habitat manipulations were not conducted.

In 1985, the Santee Preservation Society appealed the Francis Marion Land Management Plan (USDA Forest Service 1985a) on grounds, among others, that Bachman's Warblers should not be considered extirpated from the Francis Marion. The Forest Service responded by agreeing to modify the Francis Marion Land Management Plan to comply more fully with the recommendations of the 1979 biological opinion of the Fish and Wildlife Service. The Santee Preservation Society applauded the Forest Service decision to manage more actively for the species.

In August 1985, the Forest Service managers of the Francis Marion National Forest, the representative of the U.S. Fish and Wildlife Service, and personnel of the Southeastern Forest Experiment Station met to discuss progress made in carrying out the 1979 non-jeopardy opinion. As a result of this meeting, the parties agreed to carry out more fully the recommendations of the 1979 biological opinion (Black 1979) and to meet after another five years to discuss results of the efforts.

The most complete records of these proceedings are in the files of the U.S. Fish and Wildlife Service Endangered Species Field Office in Asheville, N.C., and in the files of the Wildlife, Fisheries, and Range staff unit of the U.S. Forest Service Southern Regional Office in Atlanta, Ga.

Searches

Searches of all sorts are mounted every spring in the southeastern U.S. for these, the American Birding Association's most wanted, birds (Tucker 1979). One such search was conducted for several years in the 1970's by members of the Northeast Arkansas Audubon Society in cooperation with personnel of the Big Lake National Wildlife Refuge (records in the files of the Refuge, Manila, Arkansas). The search was unsuccessful. Only one extensive, systematic search for Bachman's Warblers has been conducted, that in South Carolina, Missouri, and Arkansas in 1975-1979 (Hamel et al. 1976; Hamel and Hooper 1979a, 1979b). That search also was unsuccessful.

Future systematic searches are desirable, in spring in Alabama, Arkansas, Louisiana, Mississippi, and Tennessee, and in winter in Cuba, the Isle of Pines, and perhaps in the Bahamas and Hispaniola as well. The probability for success of any of these searches is, however, probably very low. Because the probability for success is so low, any systematic search must be well-designed and careful records of effort and coverage kept. The work of Hooper and Hamel (1974) is a guide to design of a search in the breeding season.

BEHAVIOR

General

"Typical of a warbler" may be the most apt description of the behavior of Bachman's Warblers. Stewart thought that they were typical *Vermivora* (Barnes 1954). Ficken and Ficken (1968) also considered their behavior to be typical of *Vermivora*. On migration they seem to have used available vegetation in proportion to its availability (Brewster and Chapman 1891, Scott 1890). On the breeding grounds they seem to have concentrated their foraging in the shrub layer as well as using the overstory (Widmann 1897, Wayne 1910, Tanner 1939, Barnes 1954, Chamberlain 1958). James Tanner (pers. comm., field notes for 25 May-3 June 1937), for example, noted

> "He sings from the tall trees, . . . Then every short interval he will plunge to the undergrowth for a few moments, move around a little there and then fly up to the tree tops again."

Little quantitative information comes from observations on the winter grounds. Unfortunately, no unified synthesis of the birds' behavior has been, or perhaps can be, made. Observations of the individual in Virginia in 1954 (Barnes 1954) and the one in South Carolina in 1958 (Chamberlain 1958, Dawn 1958) indicate that those birds were particularly aggressive interspecifically, against Prairie Warblers and Indigo Buntings (Passerina cyanea). Widmann (1897) noted only intraspecific aggression. Knowledge or assumptions that the birds were typically interspecifically aggressive leads to a quite different understanding of their biology and inference of their position in the swamp forest avifauna than does a view that they were not. As with so much else about these birds, speculation on this topic is all too easy.

Vocalizations

Bachman's Warbler songs have been recorded twice. Arthur Allen and Peter Paul Kellogg made a recording of the bird along Pohick Creek near Lorton, Virginia, in 1954 (Barnes 1954). Stuart Keith recorded the bird in Charleston, South Carolina, in 1958 (Chamberlain 1958). Copies of both recordings are in the collection of the Laboratory of Ornithology at Cornell University. Stein (1968a) presents a sound spectrogram of the Allen-

Kellogg recording in his analysis of vocalizations in
<u>Vermivora</u>.

A multitude of anecdotal observations of the songs
of the birds are given by virtually every early worker.
Songs most commonly are compared with those of Worm-
eating Warblers (<u>Helmitheros</u> <u>vermivorus</u>), Northern
Parulas, and Chipping Sparrows (<u>Spizella</u> <u>passerina</u>).
Wayne (1907b) reported an aberrant individual that sang
like a Prothonotary Warbler (<u>Protonotaria</u> <u>citrea</u>).
Several authors refer to the call note as a buzzy
"zeep."

Songs were given both from stationary perches and
while foraging. The birds also sang in flight, usually
giving the song just before landing (Howell 1924).
Several authors (e.g., Sprunt and Chamberlain 1970)
noted that the song had a ventriloquial quality. This
quality may have been the result of the birds' habit of
turning on the perch during a song bout, as well as the
use of flight song. I suspect that the rarity of the
species also played a role in this as well, for few
modern observers have seen enough of these birds to
have a comfortable feel for how to look for a singing
male. Henry Stevenson (pers. comm.), for example,
found Bachman's Warblers to be no more ventriloquial
than other warblers. Singing rate was variable,
possibly reflecting the stage of the nesting season
when a bird was observed. The range was from one to
ten songs per minute. Widmann (1897) presents an
interesting observation that the males with the larger
throat patches sang more vigorously earlier in his
study than did the males with smaller amounts of black
on their throats. He assumed, correctly, that the
amount of black was an indicator of the males' ages.
His observation suggests that older birds may have
arrived earlier on the breeding grounds and acquired
mates earlier than younger ones.

Foraging and Feeding

Foraging and feeding of Bachman's Warblers have been treated by few authors. Quantitative study of the foraging behavior of the birds on the breeding grounds was done by Robert Stewart (Barnes 1954) and Chamberlain (1958), who recorded the locations at which birds foraged. A composite of their results (Hamel 1981; Figure 3) showed a pattern typical of a species that sang from elevated perches, foraged to some extent in the canopy, and foraged also lower down in the shrub and herb layers. This foraging pattern is not unlike that of either Swainson's Warblers or Prairie Warblers (Hamel 1981). Tanner (pers. comm.) came to the same conclusion. The birds were said by several authors to glean leaves, clumps of dead leaves, and flowers. These behaviors are also typical of their presumed closest relatives, V. chrysoptera and V. pinus (Ficken and Ficken 1968). Rate of foraging varied from extremely active (Atkins in Scott 1890a) to leisurely (Brewster 1891), suggesting that individual birds were under different motivations at different times when observed.

Food of the birds on the breeding grounds consisted primarily of insects and other small arthropods, with a small amount of seeds that may have been taken incidental to the capture of insects and their larvae. Meanley and Mitchell (1958) analyzed the contents of 14 stomachs taken from Alabama, Arkansas, Florida, and Missouri in 1905-1916.

Foraging behavior on the winter grounds in Cuba has not been studied in detail. Barbour (1923) quotes Gundlach (1893) to the effect that the birds foraged in and about the flowers of Hibiscus tiliaceus shrubs and trees. The birds may have sought nectar as well as insects. The birds' curved bills suggest that some such specialization is possible, although none has been demonstrated. I paraphrase Orlando Garrido's comments (pers. comm.), as follows:

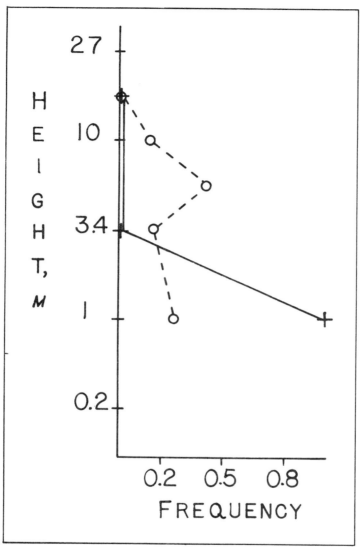

Figure 3. Behavior-height profile for Bachman's
Warbler. Dashed line indicates distribution of all
behaviors observed, solid line indicates that of
foraging observations only. Data taken from Stewart
(in Barnes 1954) and Chamberlain, E. B. (1958).

You mentioned that the curved bill of the warbler may represent a "specialty." This could be, or not. Our endemic _Teretistris fernandinae_ has a curved bill, and this tool is used for all kinds of purposes. She fills the ecological niches of several migratory warblers . . . She travels in groups, and practically "combs" the territory, from ground to above 4 meters high, assuming the feeding behavior of several other species. . . . As a _Vermivora_, in their transit grounds here, _V. pinus_, _V. chrysoptera_, and _V. peregrina_ are middle or high level feeders. However, Bachman's Warbler apparently feeds in the three situations; I have found her at low stages (one meter above the ground); about two and a half meters; and Gundlach mentions feeding on flowers of majagua, which means that she goes to high levels also. My three encounters with her were in trees with small leaves; however, the majagua trees have broad leaves. There is no doubt that she feeds on honey, just as _Dendroica tigrina_ at least. I have seen _V. peregrina_ and _V. chrysoptera_ on flowers of majagua as well. They may also get some insects as well. I have not observed any feedings or aggressive display on my encounters with _V. bachmanii_. _Teretistris_ sometimes travels in mixed flocks with other warblers and _Vireo gundlachii_ when foraging. When I saw _V. bachmanii_ for the first time in Zapata, a flock of Chillinas [_Teretistris fernandinae_] was around. The warbler was within one meter of my head, and I was sitting on the ground. She soon disappeared among the bushes after I stood up . . . The second one was still on a branch for some time. The tree was separate from the rest of the vegetation. She flew a distance away to cover. The one found in Soroa was in the woods, about 3 meters from the ground on a tree near the road. The hill was about 300 m elevation (Sierra del Rosario).

Sciple (1950) collected a female along the Mississippi coast during a 1949 survey for avian encephalomyelitis. The bird had no parasites in its blood.

GEOGRAPHICAL DISTRIBUTION

A very large number of the references in the bibliography record only occurrence of Bachman's Warblers. Each of them is listed under the appropriate Caribbean island or individual state in U.S. Most of the references record actual occurrence of the birds but a few report negative data (e.g. Hooper and Hamel 1979b, Lane 1981), or expectations (e.g. Ganier 1917, 1933; the birds have never actually been recorded in Tennessee).

In several cases confusion exists concerning occurrence of the birds or the interpretation of reports. This confusion is particularly true concerning records from Georgia, Illinois, Indiana, and the Isle of Pines. Thus the early records for Illinois (Ridgway 1874, 1878) are perplexing. Ridgway would certainly have known the significance of his find [it predates the generally acclaimed "rediscovery" of Galbraith (1886) by almost ten years], yet he failed to do more than note a sight record. Confusion over records from Georgia is more substantial. Bailey's (1883) report of a clutch of eggs is generally discounted (Wayne 1910b), but Wayne's (1912) attack on the report by Hoxie (1911) may or may not have been justified. [Fargo (1934) believed that that attack caused Hoxie to forsake ornithology.] The Indiana specimen reported by Butler (1899) cannot be found and the report by Wilson (1918) may be questionable (Mumford and Keller 1975). A similar situation exists with the single record from the Isle of Pines. Read (1909a, 1909b, 1911, 1913, Reed 1911) took a specimen which he kept in his personal collection. The bird was listed in each of his reports and subsequently destroyed in a flood with the rest of his collection and notes. Todd (1916) then listed the bird as hypothetical for the Isle of Pines.

Recent sight records pose another problem. Our present knowledge of the rarity of the species leads to a much closer scrutiny of these records than was given to earlier reports. All known published reports are included in the bibliography, without qualification. A sample of the possible disagreement over validity of reports can be seen by comparing the evaluations of Hamel and Hooper (1979a) with those of Shuler et al. (1978). A critical reexamination of some other sight records from earlier times would probably yield similar uncertainty.

LITERATURE CITED

These papers were cited in this chapter but do not directly mention Bachman's Warblers.

Allen, T. F. H., and T. B. Starr.
    1982. Hierarchy: Perspectives for ecological complexity. 310 p. University of Chicago Press, Chicago.

Banks, R.
    1976. "Extation." Science 191(4233):1217, 1292.

Bradley, J. T.
    1972. The climate of Florida. June 1972. In Climates of the states. vol. 1. Eastern states. 1974. pp. 45-70. U.S. Dept. Commerce, National Oceanic and Atmospheric Administration.

Cry, G. W.
   1965. Tropical cyclones of the North Atlantic
   Ocean: Tracks and frequencies of hurricanes and
   tropical storms, 1871-1963. 148 p. U.S. Dept.
   Commerce, Weather Bureau, Technical Paper 55.

Flint, R. F.
   1957. Glacial and Pleistocene geology. 553 p.
   John Wiley & Sons, Inc., N. Y.

Forsythe, D., and W. R. Tyler.
   1982. Breeding bird census of swamp hardwood forest
   in coastal South Carolina. American Birds
   36(1):59-60.

Holder, T.
   1970. Disappearing wetlands in eastern Arkansas.
   72 p. Arkansas Planning Commission, Little Rock.

Horner, R. S.
   1973. History and genealogy of Cardwell, Buffalo
   Township, Missouri. 486 p. Coursey Printing Co.,
   Kennett, Missouri.

Huntington, J. L. and T. Barbour.
   1936. The birds at Soledad, Cuba, after a
   hurricane. Auk 53:436-437.

Kochtitsky, O.
   1957. The story of a busy life. 173 p. Ramfre
   Press, Cape Girardeau, Missouri.

Lanyon, W. E. and F. B. Gill.
   1964. Spectrographic analysis of variation in the
   songs of a population of Blue-winged Warblers
   (Vermivora pinus). American Museum Novitates, No.
   2176:1-18.

Nice, M. M.
   1941. The role of territory in bird life. American
   Midland Naturalist 26:441-487.

Nolen, J. H.
   1913. Missouri's swamps and overflowed lands and
   their reclamation. Report to the 47th Missouri
   General Assembly. Hugh Stephens Printing Co.,
   Jefferson City, Missouri.

Shugart, H. H.
   1984. A theory of forest dynamics. 278 p.
   Springer-Verlag, New York.

Tannehill, I. R.
   1945. Hurricanes. 275 p. Princeton University
   Press, Princeton, N. J.

Wiens, J. A.
   1977. On competition and variable environments.
   American Scientist 65:590-597.

Williams, J. S.
   1975. Old times in west Tennessee. 295 p.
   Unigraphic, Inc., Evansville, Ind. [Reprint of
   1873 edition published by W. G. Cheeney, Memphis,
   Tennessee]

Part 2. Literature of Bachman's Warbler

This bibliography contains all of the primary, i.e. original presentations of new data, and secondary, i.e. summarizations or evaluations of original data, ornithological papers and books published through 31 August 1985. It was compiled by careful search of the following sources:

1. Indices of major English language ornithological journals and the <u>Zoological Record</u>.

2. Major works treating the birds of the Americas and the world.

3. Bird books and bird journals produced in states in the historical breeding range of the species.

4. Unpublished government and other reports concerning this species.

5. Major works on endangered species.

6. General treatises on ornithology.

7. Literature cited sections of all of the above.

In addition, a variety of other leads were pursued. Only a sample of the large number of popular endangered species books is included. I stopped short of including newspaper articles except where no other primary source for the same information was available. Where the information concerning Bachman's Warbler is substantially different in different editions of a work, each edition is listed. Otherwise only the most recent is listed. Where works have been reprinted, the edition listed is the one I examined, even when it was not an original one. It was possible to check the accuracy of approximately 90% of the citations by reexamining copies of the original works.

In several cases works bear directly upon each other, as reviews, rebuttals, alternate interpretations, or the like. In such cases, annotations point the reader to related views. Examples include works that pertain to the controversy over management of National Forest lands in I'On Swamp, Charleston County, South Carolina, in the 1970's and 1980's.

Five hundred and one papers are listed in this bibliography. Of these, 206 (41%) are referenced under more than one subject heading, and 104 (21%) under more than two. Number of subject headings referenced is one crude guide to the importance of a paper. Twenty-four papers are referenced under six or more subject headings, as follows:

14 times--Widmann 1897;

11 times--Howell 1928, Stevenson 1972b;

10 times--Barnes 1954, Dingle 1963;

 9 times--Imhof 1976;

 8 times--Brewster 1891, King 1978, Stevenson 1975, Wayne 1907a, Wayne 1910a;

 7 times--Dawn 1958, Evenden et al. 1977, Sprunt and Chamberlain 1970, Stevenson 1938;

 6 times--Arnow 1908, Chamberlain 1958, Embody 1907, Griscom and Sprunt 1979, Hamel 1981, Potter et al. 1980, Scott 1890a, Sprunt 1954a, Stevenson 1978.

A second estimate of the importance of a particular paper is its appearance in Chapter 1 of this work. Papers cited there contribute, in my judgment, important information to an understanding of the

biology and history of the species. The large number
of references to Widmann (1897) in the third section
and the large number of citations of the work in the
first section support and reflect my opinion that that
is the single most important first-hand account of the
Bachman's Warbler yet written.

Bachman's Warbler singing 15 m up in lower canopy of
Longleaf Pine, 1958, Charleston Co., S. C.
Photo courtesy of Walter Dawn.

Alphabetical Listing by Author

Aldrich, J. W.
   1970. Before it is too late. In Birds in our
      lives. p. 376-393. A. Stefferud and A. L. Nel-
      son, eds. Arco Publ. Co., Inc., New York.

Allen, J. A.
   1888. Notes on Louisiana birds. Auk 5:324-325.

Allen, J. A.
   1893. The geographical origin and distribution of
      North American birds, considered in relation to
      faunal areas of North America. Auk 10(2):97-150.

Allison, A.
   1904. The birds of west Baton Rouge Parish, Louisi-
      ana. Auk 21:472-484.

Amadon, D.
   1953. Migratory birds of relict distribution: some
      inferences. Auk 70(4):461-469.

Am. Ornithol. Union
   1886. Code of Nomenclature and check-list of North
      American birds. 392 p. Am. Ornithol. Union, New
      York.

Am. Ornithol. Union
   1909. Fifteenth supplement to the American Orni-
      thologists Union check-list of North American
      birds. Auk 26:294-303.

Am. Ornithol. Union
   1944a. Nineteenth supplement to the American Orni-
      thologists Union check-list of North American
      birds. Auk 61:441-464.

Am. Ornithol. Union
   1944b. Report of the American Ornithologists Union
      committee on bird protection for 1943. Auk
      61:622-635.

Am. Ornithol. Union
   1957. Checklist of North American birds. 5th ed.
      691 p. Am. Ornithol. Union, Baltimore.

Am. Ornithol. Union
  1963. Report of the committee on bird protection,
    1962. Auk 80:352-364.

Am. Ornithol. Union
  1975. Report of the committee on conservation. Auk
    92(4,suppl.):1B-16B.

Am. Ornithol. Union
  1978. Proceedings of the ninety-fifth stated meet-
    ing of the American Ornithologists' Union. Auk
    95(1, Suppl.):1AA-19AA.

Am. Ornithol. Union·
  1983. Check-list of North American birds. 6th ed.
    877 p. Am. Ornithol. Union, Lawrence, Kansas.

Arnow, I. F.
  1908. Bachman's Warbler in Camden Co. and breeding
    in Chatham Co., Georgia. Auk 25:479. SEE: Wayne
    1912.

Audubon, J. J.
  1831-1834. The birds of America. vol. 2. 100
    color plates. J. J. Audubon, London.

Audubon, J. J.
  1834. Ornithological biography. vol. 2. Adam and
    Charles Black, Edinburgh.

Audubon, J. J.
  1839. Synopsis of the birds of America. 359 p.
    Adam and Charles Black, Edinburgh.

Audubon, J. J.
  1841. Birds of America. vol 2. 205 p. 70 color
    plates. J. J. Audubon, New York.

Audubon, J. J.
  1966. The original watercolor paintings by John
    James Audubon for the birds of America. 2 vols.
    431 color plates. Heritage, New York.

Averill, C. K.
  1920. Migration and physical proportions: a prelim-
    inary study. Auk 37:572-579.

Averill, C. K.
  1924. Vigor, distribution, and pigmentation of the
    egg. Condor 26:140-143.

Baerg, W. J.
  1951. Birds of Arkansas, rev ed. Univ. Ark. Agric.
  Exp. Stn. Bull. 258. 188 p.

Bailey, F. M.
  1933. Some of the birds of the Mammoth Cave region.
  Am. Midl. Nat. 14(5):463-574.

Bailey, H. B.
  1883. Memoranda of a collection of eggs from Georgia. Bull. Nutt. Ornithol. Club 8:37-43.

Bailey, H. H.
  1913. The birds of Virginia. 362 p. J. P. Bell,
  Lynchburg, Va.

Bailey, H. H.
  1925. Birds of Florida. 146 p. Williams & Wil-
  kins, Baltimore.

Baird, S. F.
  1858. Birds of North America. Report of explora-
  tions and surveys of a railroad route to the
  Pacific Ocean. Part 2. 1005 p. Beverly Tucker,
  Washington, D. C.

Baird, S. F.
  1862. Catalogue of North American birds, chiefly in
  the museum of the Smithsonian Institution.
  (1859). Smithson. Misc. Coll. II. no. 182.

Baird, S. F.
  1864. Review of American birds in the museum of the
  Smithsonian Insti- tution. pt. I. North and Middle America. 478 p. Smithson. Misc. Coll. 181.

Baird, S. F.
  1867. The distribution and migration of North American birds. Ibis 11:257-293.

Baird, S. F., T. M. Brewer, and R. Ridgway
  1874. History of North American birds. Vol. 1.
  Land Birds. 596 p. Little, Brown, and Co., Boston.

Balboa, P. F.
  1941. Las aves de Cuba. 215 p. Cultural, S. A.,
  Habana.

Barber, R. D.
    1985. A recent record of the Bachman's Warbler in
    Florida. Florida Field Naturalist 13:64-66.

Barbour, R. W., C. T. Peterson, D. Rust, H. E. Sha-
    dowen, and A. L. Whitt, Jr.
    1973. Kentucky birds, a finding guide. 306 p.
    Univ. Ky. Press, Lexington.

Barbour, T.
    1923. The birds of Cuba. Mem. Nutt. Ornithol.
    Club 6, 141 p.

Barbour, T.
    1943. Cuban ornithology. Mem. Nutt. Ornithol. Club
    9, 144 p.

Barnes, I. R.
    1954. A new look at Bachman's Warbler. Atlantic
    Nat. 10:18-30.

Bass, K. H.
    1979a. A trip to I'On Swamp in 1978. Birding
    11:270-274.

Bass, K. H.
    1979b. I'On Swamp revisited in 1979. Birding
    11:275.

Bassett, A. S.
    1941. A late specimen of Bachman's Warbler from
    Georgia. Oriole 6:38.

Baumgartner, F. M.
    1951. Southern Great Plains region. Audubon Field
    Notes 5:263-265.

Baumgartner, F. M.
    1960. Southern Great Plains region. Audubon Field
    Notes 14:398-401.

Baumgartner, F. M.
    1963. Southern Great Plains region. Audubon Field
    Notes 17:414-415.

Baynard, O.
    1942. Birds of Hillsborough River State Park (Flo-
    rida). p. 1-6. In Birds, Mammals, Reptiles and
    Amphibians of Hillsborough River State Park. J.
    A. Stevenson, ed.

Berger, A. J.
    1961. Bird study. 389 p. J. Wiley & Sons, N. Y.

Beyer, G. E.
    1900. The avifauna of Louisiana. Proc. La. Soc.
    Nat. 1897-1899: 75-120.

Black, K.
    1979. [Letter to Lawrence Whitfield, July 2, 1979.]
    4 p. [This is the final Biological Opinion of the
    USDI Fish and Wildlife Service to the USDA Forest
    Service concerning management of the Francis
    Marion National Forest and Bachman's Warblers.
    (On file at R. M. Cooper Library, Clemson Univ.,
    Clemson, S. C.)]

Blair, W. F., A. P. Blair, P. Brodkorb, F. R. Cagle,
    and G. A. Moore
    1968. Vertebrates of the United States, 2nd ed.
    616 p. McGraw-Hill, N. Y.

Blake, E. R.
    1948. Middle-western region. Audubon Field Notes
    2:180-181.

Bohlen, H. D.
    1978. An annotated check-list of the birds of Illi-
    nois. Ill. State Mus., Pop. Science Ser., vol.
    9. 156 p.

Bonaparte, C. L.
    1838. Geographic and comparative list of the birds
    of Europe and North America. 67 p. Van Voorst,
    London.

Bonaparte, C. L.
    1854. Conspectus systematis ornithologiae. Extr.
    from Ann. des Sci. Nat. 4(I):105-152.

Bond, J.
    1936. Birds of the West Indies. 456 p. Acad. Nat.
    Sci. Phila., Philadelphia.

Bond, J.
    1945a. The wood warblers. Audubon 47:67-73.

Bond, J.
    1956. Check-list of birds of the West Indies. 4th
    ed. 214 p. Acad. Nat. Sci. Phila., Philadel-
    phia.

49

Bond, J.
    1957.   North American wood warblers in the West
    Indies.   Audubon 59:20-23.

Bond, J.
    1971.   Birds of the West Indies. 2nd ed.   256 p.
    Houghton Mifflin, Boston.

Bondeson, P.
    1977.   North American bird songs - a world of music.
    254 p.   Scandinavian Science Press, Klampenborg,
    Denmark.

Bonhote, J. L.
    1903.   Bird migration at some of the Bahama
    lighthouses.   Auk 20:169-179.

Booth, E. S.
    1962.   Birds of the East.   335 p.   Outdoor Pict.,
    Escondido, Calif.

Boucard, A.
    1876.   Catalogus avium hucusque descriptarum.   352
    p.   London.

Brasher, R.
    1962.   Birds and trees of North America.   vol. 4.
    62 p.   211 color plates.   Rowman and Littlefield,
    N. Y.   [Originally published by the author as a
    limited edition of 100 copies in 1932.]

Brewer, R.
    1958.   Some corrections to "A distributional check
    list of the birds of Illinois."   Audubon Bull.
    (Ill.) 106:9.   [Not seen, _fide_ Graber et al.
    1983.]

Brewer, T. M.
    1860.   List of the birds of Cuba.   Proc. Boston Soc.
    Nat. Hist.   7:305-308.

Brewster, W.
    1886.   An ornithological reconnaissance in western
    North Carolina.   Auk 3:94-112.

Brewster, W.
    1887.   An overlooked specimen of Bachman's Warbler.
    Auk 4:165.

Brewster, W.
    1891. Notes on Bachman's Warbler (*Helminthophila bachmani*). Auk 8(2):149-157.

Brewster, W.
    1905. Notes on the breeding of Bachman's Warbler, Helminthophila <u>bachmanii</u> (Aud.), near Charleston, South Carolina, with a description of the first plumage of the species. Auk 22:392-394.

Brewster, W., and F. M. Chapman
    1891. Notes on the birds of the lower Suwanee River. Auk 8:125-138.

Brimley, C. S.
    1891. Bachman's Warbler (*Helminthophila bachmani*) at Raleigh, North Carolina. Auk 8:316-317.

Brimley, C. S.
    1917. Thirty-two years of bird migration at Raleigh, North Carolina. Auk 34:296-308.

Brimley, C. S.
    1930. The birds of Raleigh, North Carolina. J. Elisha Mitchell Soc. 46:74-85.

Brooks, M.
    1946. Bull's Island. Audubon 48:322-329.

Brudenell-Bruce, P. G. C.
    1975. The birds of New Providence and the Bahamas. 142 p. Collins, London.

Buchheister, C. W.
    1974. Gift of awareness. S. C. Wildlife 21(4):34-39.

Buhrman, C. B.
    1977. Endangered Pronunciations. Birding 9(4):164-165.

Bull, J. L.
    1958. The changing seasons: a summary of the nesting season. Audubon Field Notes 12:392-395.

Bull, J. L., and J. Farrand, Jr.
    1977. The Audubon Society field guide to North American birds, eastern region. 775 p. Alfred A. Knopf, Inc., N. Y.

Burleigh, T. D.
    1944. The bird life of the Gulf Coast region of
    Mississippi. La. State Univ., Occas. Pap. Mus.
    Zool. 20:329-490.

Burleigh, T. D.
    1957. Occurrence of Bachman's Warbler (*Vermivora
    bachmani*) in northern Mississippi in June. Auk
    74:94-95.

Burleigh, T. D.
    1958. Georgia birds. 746 p. Univ. Okla. Press,
    Norman, Okla.

Burns, F. L.
    1908. Alexander Wilson. II. The mystery of the
    small-headed flycatcher. Wilson Bull. 20:63-78.

Burton, E. M.
    1970. Supplement. In South Carolina birdlife, rev.
    ed. p. 573-642. A. Sprunt, Jr., and E. B. Cham-
    berlain. Univ. S. C. Press, Columbia.

Butler, A. W.
    1900. Notes on Indiana birds. Proc. Ind. Acad.
    Sci. 1899:149-151.

Butler, A. W.
    1934. Does Bachman's Warbler winter in Florida?
    Auk 51:89.

Campbell, B., Roundtable ed.
    1977. Roundtable: Answering environmental back-
    lash. S. C. Wildlife 24(4):58-59.

Carolina Bird Club
    1950. Annual meeting held at Charleston. Chat
    14:33-36.

Carolina Bird Club
    1963. News and comments. Chat 27(3):59.

Chamberlain, B. R.
    1958. Southern Atlantic Coast region. Audubon
    Field Notes 12:404-405.

Chamberlain, B. R.
    1959. Southern Atlantic Coast region. Audubon
    Field Notes 13:360-362.

Chamberlain, B. R.
   1960a. The 1960 spring count. Chat 24:65-73, 77.

Chamberlain, B. R.
   1960b. Southern Atlantic Coast region. Audubon
   Field Notes 14:377-379.

Chamberlain, B. R.
   1961a. The 1961 spring count. Chat 25:50-63.

Chamberlain, B. R.
   1961b. Southern Atlantic Coast region. Audubon
   Field Notes 15:399-402.

Chamberlain, B. R.
   1961c. Southern Atlantic Coast region. Audubon
   Field Notes 15:458-461.

Chamberlain, B. R.
   1962. Southern Atlantic Coast region. Audubon
   Field Notes 16:396-398.

Chamberlain, E. B.
   1958. Bachman's Warbler in South Carolina. Chat
   22:73-74, 77.

Chamberlain, E. B.
   1959. [Note in "Briefs for the Files."] Chat
   23:69.

Chamberlain, E. B.
   1968. Birds of the Francis Marion National Forest.
   32 p. USDA For. Serv. South. Reg., Atlanta.

Chamberlain, E. B.
   1974. Rare and endangered birds of the southern
   National Forests. 108 p. USDA For. Serv. South.
   Reg., Atlanta.

Chamberlain, E. B.
   1978. Field list of South Carolina birds. 10 p.
   Charleston, S. C., Natural History Society.

Chamberlain, E. B., and B. R. Chamberlain
   1948. Carolina region. Audubon Field Notes
   2:172-174.

Chapman, F. M.
   1889. *Helminthophila bachmani* on the east coast of
   Florida. Auk 6:278-279.

53

Chapman, F. M.
    1966. Handbook of birds of eastern North America.
    2nd rev. ed.   581 p.   Dover Reprints, N. Y.
    [Reprint of 1939 edition published by D.   Appleton
    Century Co., N. Y.]

Chapman, F. M.
    1968. The warblers of North America.   307 p.   Dover
    Reprints, N. Y. [Reprint of 1917 edition pub-
    lished by Appleton, N. Y.]

Chapman, F. M., and C. A. Reed
    1903. Color key to North American birds.   312 p.
    Doubleday, Page and Co., N. Y.

Childs, J. L., ed.
    1906. Ornithological collection of John Lewis
    Childs, Floral Park, N. Y. Warbler (ser.
    2)2:66-106.

Choate, E. A.
    1973. The dictionary of American bird names.   261
    p. Gambit, Boston.

Clark, A. H.
    1938. Notes on Virginia birds.   Raven 9:29-31.

Clements, J. F.
    1974. Birds of the world: a checklist.   524 p.   Two
    Continents Publ. Group Ltd., N. Y.

Cohen, M.
    1976. Bachman's Warbler: the last of a living
    thing? Natl. Wildl. Fed. Conserv. News
    41(13):2-5.

Coleman, R. H.
    1961a. [Note in "Briefs for the Files."]   Chat
    25(2):42.

Coleman, R. H.
    1961b. [Note in "Briefs for the Files."]   Chat
    25(4):96.

Collins, H. H., Jr.
    1960. Abridged Bent's life histories of North Amer-
    ican birds. vol. 2. Land birds.   374 p.   Harper
    & Bros., N. Y.

Cooke, W. W.
    1904. Distribution and migration of North American warblers. USDA Div. Biol. Surv. Bull. 18, 142 p.

Cooke, W. W.
    1905. The winter ranges of the warblers (Mniotiltidae). Auk 22:296-299.

Cooke, W. W.
    1906. The migration of warblers: fourteenth paper. Bird Lore 8:26-27.

Cooper, J. E., S. S. Robinson, J. B. Funderberg, eds.
    1977. Endangered and threatened plants and animals of North Carolina. 444 p. N. C. State Mus. Nat. Hist., Raleigh, N. C.

Cory, C. B.
    1885. List of birds of the West Indies including the Bahama Islands and the Greater and Lesser Antilles, excepting the islands of Tobago and Trinidad. 34 p. Estes & Lauriat, Boston.

Cory, C. B.
    1886. The birds of the West Indies, including the Bahama Islands, the Greater and Lesser Antilles, excepting the islands of Tobago and Trinidad. Auk 3:1-59.

Cory, C. B.
    1889. Birds of the West Indies. 324 p. Estes & Lauriat, Boston.

Cory, C. B.
    1892. Catalog of West Indian birds. 163 p. C. B. Cory, Boston.

Coues, E.
    1869. Synopsis of the birds of South Carolina. Proc. Bost. Soc. Nat. Hist. 12:104-127.

Coues, E.
    1870. The natural history of *Quiscalus major*. Ibis 6:367-378.

Coues, E.
    1878. Birds of the Colorado valley. U. S. Geol. Surv. Territ. Misc. Publ. 11:1-807.

Coues, E.
1882. The Coues check list of North American birds, 2nd ed., rev. 165 p. Estes and Lauriat, Boston.

Coues, E.
1903. Key to North American birds. 5th ed. vol. 1. 535 p. Dana Estes, Boston.

Cox, J. A.
1975. The endangered ones. 224 p. Crown Publ., N. Y.

Culler, J.
1971. Our endangered ones. S. C. Wildlife 18(4):12-17.

Cunningham, J. W.
1940. Birds of the southeast. Bluebird 7(9):63-64.

Curry-Lindahl, K.
1972. Let them live. 394 p. Wm. Morrow & Co., N. Y.

Curtis, R. L., Jr.
1978. A representative sample of ongoing and planned nongame bird research in the southeastern region United States. p. 166-176. In Proceed. workshop management of southern forests for nongame birds. p. 166-176. R. M. DeGraaf, Tech. Coord. USDA For. Serv., Gen. Tech. Rep. SE-14. Southeast. For. Exp. Stn., Asheville, N. C.

Cutts, E.
1964. Rev. John Bachman's unpredictable warbler. Frontiers (April, 1964):112-114.

Davie, O.
1898. Nests and eggs of North American birds. 5th ed. 548 p. David McKay, Philadelphia.

Dawn, W.
1958. An anomalous Bachman's Warbler. Atlantic Nat. 13(4):229-232.

Dawn, W.
1962. Rare warbler of southern swamps is more often heard than seen. Natural Hist. 71:41-43.

Deane, R.
   1929. Some letters of Bachman to Audubon. Auk
   46:177-185.

Deignan, H. G.
   1961. Type specimens of birds in the United States
   National Museum. U. S. Nat. Mus. Bull. 221, 718
   p.

Denton, J. F., and B. R. Chamberlain
   1950. Southern Atlantic Coast region. Audubon
   Field Notes 4:238-239.

Denton, J. F., and M. Hopkins, Jr.
   1969. Pocket checklist: Georgia birds. Georgia
   Ornithol Soc., Atlanta.

Denton, J. F., W. W. Baker, L. B. Davenport, Jr., M. N.
   Hopkins, Jr., and C. S. Robbins
   1977. Annotated checklist of Georgia birds. Occas.
   Publ. No. 6, 60 p. Georgia Ornithol. Soc.,
   Atlanta.

Dick, J. H.
   1956. [Drawing of male Bachman's Warbler.] Audubon
   Field Notes 10(4):front cover.

Dick, J. H.
   1958. [Photograph of singing male Bachman's Warbler.] Chat 22(4):front cover.

Dickson, J. G.
   1978. Forest bird communities of the bottomland
   hardwoods. In Proceed. workshop management of
   southern forests for nongame birds. p. 66-73. R.
   M. DeGraaf, Tech. Coord. USDA For. Serv., Gen.
   Tech. Rep. SE-14. Southeast. For. Exp. Stn.,
   Asheville, N. C.

Dingle, E. von S.
   1963. *Vermivora bachmanii* (Audubon). Bachman's Warbler. *In* Life histories of North American wood
   warblers. Part I. p. 67- 74. A. C. Bent, ed.
   Dover Reprints, N. Y. [Originally published in
   1953 as U. S. Natl. Mus. Bull. 203.]

Drury, W. H.
   1974. Rare species. Biol. Cons. 6:162-169.

Eagar, D. C., and R. M. Hatcher, eds.
    1980. Tennessee's Rare Wildlife. 335 p. Tenn.
    Dept. Cons. and Tenn. Wildl. Res. Agency, Nash-
    ville.

Embody, G. C.
    1907. Bachman's Warbler breeding in Logan County,
    Kentucky. Auk 24:41-42.

Evenden, F. G., D. B. Marshall, and W. D. Zeedyk
    1976a. Preliminary report of the Bachman's Warbler
    panel. Unpublished report. 7 p. [On file at R.
    M. Cooper Libr., Clemson Univ., Clemson, S. C.]
    SEE: Harrison et al. 1977.

Evenden, F. G., D. B. Marshall, and W. D. Zeedyk
    1976b. Report of the Bachman's Warbler panel.
    Unpublished report. 9 p. [On file at R. M.
    Cooper Libr., Clemson Univ., Clemson, S. C.]

Evenden, F. G., D. B. Marshall, and W. D. Zeedyk
    1977. Revised final report of the Bachman's Warbler
    panel. Unpublished report. 30 p. [On file at R.
    M. Cooper Libr., Clemson Univ., Clemson, S. C.]

Faaborg, J. R., and J. W. Terborgh
    1980. Patterns of migration in the West Indies. In
    Migrant birds in the Neotropics: Ecology, behav-
    ior, distribution, and conservation. p. 157-163.
    A. Keast and E. S. Morton, eds. Smithsonian
    Inst. Press, Washington, D. C.

Fargo, W. G.
    1934. Walter John Hoxie. Wilson Bull. 46:169-196.

Farrand, J., Jr., ed.
    1983. The Audubon Society master guide to birding.
    vol. 3. Warblers to sparrows. 400 p. A. A.
    Knopf, N. Y.

Faver, A. R.
    1953. Rare warblers in the Carolinas. Chat
    17(2):30-33.

Fawks, E.
    1936. Warblers of Rock Island County in 1935.
    Audubon Bull. (Ill.) 26:40-41. [Not seen, fide
    Graber et al. 1983.]

Ficken, M. S. and R. W. Ficken.
    1968. Ecology of Blue-winged Warblers, Golden-
    winged Warblers, and some other Vermivora.
    American Midland Naturalist 79:311-319.

Figgins, J. D.
    1945. Birds of Kentucky. 366 p. Univ. Ky. Press,
    Lexington.

Fink, L. C.
    1978. CBC Roundtable: more Bachman's Warbler publi-
    cations. Chat 42(1):8.

Fisher, J.
    1960. Bird species in danger of extinction. Inter-
    nat. Zoo Yearbook 2:280-287.

Fisher, J., N. Simon, and J. Vincent
    1969. The red book: wildlife in danger. 368 p.
    Collins, London.

Florida Game and Freshwater Fish Comm.
    1976. Cross Florida barge canal restudy report:
    endangered, threatened, rare, special concern,
    status undetermined and biologically sensitive
    species, submitted to U. S. Fish and Serv. 267 p.
    U. S. Army Corps Eng., Jacksonville, Fl.

Forbush, E. H., and J. B. May
    1939. Natural history of the birds of eastern and
    central North America. 554 p. Houghton Mifflin,
    Boston.

Forsythe, D. M.
    1978. Birds. In An annotated checklist of the
    biota of the coastal zone of South Carolina. p.
    277-295. R. G. Zingmark, ed. Univ. S. C. Press,
    Columbia.

Funkhouser, W. D.
    1925. Wildlife in Kentucky. 385 p. Ky. Geol.
    Surv., Geol. Rep. Ser. 6, vol. 16, Frankfort, Ky.

Gaddy, L. L.
    1979. Natural resources inventory of Congaree Swamp
    National Monument and environs. 116 p. USDI Nat.
    Park Serv., Denver Serv. Center, Denver, Colo.

Galbraith, C. S.
   1888. Bachman's Warbler (*Helminthophila bachmani*) in
   Louisiana. Auk 5:323.

Ganier, A.
   1916. Notes on the breeding warblers of Tennessee.
   Wilson Bull. 28:138-143.

Ganier, A.
   1917. Preliminary list of birds of Tennessee. 28
   p. Dep. Game and Fish of Tenn., Nashville.

Ganier, A. F.
   1933. A distributional list of the birds of Tennes-
   .see. Tenn. Avif. No. 1. 64 p. Tenn. Ornithol.
   Soc., Nashville, Tenn.

Garrido, O. H.
   1985. Cuban endangered birds. In Neotropical
   ornithology. pp. 992-999. Buckley, P. A., M. S.
   Foster, E. S. Morton, R. S. Ridgely, and F. G.
   Buckley, eds. American Ornithologists' Union,
   Ornithological Monograph 36.

Garrido, O. H., and F. Garcia Montana
   1975. Catalogo de las aves de Cuba. 149 p. Acad.
   Ciencias de Cuba, Habana.

Gault, B. T.
   1922. Checklist of the birds of Illinois. 80 p.
   Ill. Audubon Soc., Chicago.

Gauthreaux, S. A., Jr.
   1973. The changing seasons: spring migration, 1973.
   Am. Birds 27:743-748.

Gauthreaux, S. A., Jr.
   1976. [Painting of Bachman's Warblers.] S. C.
   Wildlife 23(2):inside back cover.

Gauthreaux, S. A., Jr.
   1977. [Painting of Bachman's Warblers.] Wilson
   Bull.89(3):frontis- piece.

Gee, J. P.
   1977. The changing seasons. Am. Birds
   31(5):966-971.

Geffen, A. M.
    1978. A birdwatcher's guide to the eastern United
    States. 346 p. Barron's, Woodbury, N. Y.

Geibel, C. G.
    1875. Thesaurus ornithologiae. vol. 2. 787 p. F.
    A. Brockhaus, Leipzig.

George, W. G.
    1971. Vanished and endangered birds of Illinois: A
    new 'black list' and 'red list.' Audubon Bull.
    (Ill.) 158:2-11. [Not seen, fide Graber et al.
    1983.]

Gibbes, L. R.
    1848. Catalogue of the fauna of South Carolina.
    Appendix. In Report on the Geology of South Caro-
    lina. p. i-xxiv. M. Tuomey, compiler. A. S.
    Johnston, Columbia, S. C.

Gilbert, W. M.
    1983. Flight song and song flight in the Orange-
    crowned Warbler. Condor 85:113.

Gochfeld, M.
    1974. Status of the genus *Vermivora* (Aves Parulidae)
    in the Greater Antilles with new records from
    Jamaica and Puerto Rico. Carib. J. Sci.
    14(3-4):177-181.

Gochfeld, M.
    1979. Wintering ranges of migrant warblers of
    eastern North America. Amer. Birds 33:742-745.

Golsan, L. S., and E. G. Holt
    1914. Birds of Autauga and Montgomery counties,
    Alabama. Auk 31:212-235.

Goodwin, H. A.
    1974. Here today . . . gone tomorrow. Natl. Wild-
    life 12(3):29-31.

Graber, J. W., R. R. Graber, and E. L. Kirk.
    1983. Illinois birds: Wood warblers. Ill. Nat.
    Hist. Surv., Biol. Notes 118, 144 p.

Gray, G. R.
    1849. The genera of birds. Vol. 1. 300 p. Long-
    man, Brown, Green, and Longmans, London.

Gray, G. R.
   1869. Handlist of genera and species of birds, dis-
   tinguishing those contained in the British Museum.
   Pt. 1. Accipitres, Fissirostres, Tenuirostres,
   and Dentirostres. 404 p. Taylor & Francis, London.

Greene, E. R.
   1933. Birds of the Atlanta, Georgia, area, distribution, migration and nesting. Bull. Ga. Soc.
   Nat. 2:1-6.

Greene, E. R., W. W. Griffin, E. P. Odum, H. L. Stod-
   dard and I. R. Tomkins ،
   1945. Birds of Georgia. Ga. Ornithol. Soc. Occas.
   Publ. No. 2. 111 p. Univ. Ga. Press, Athens.

Greenway, J. C., Jr.
   1958. Extinct and vanishing birds of the world.
   518 p. Amer. Comm. for Internat. Wildl. Protection, N. Y.

Griffin, W. W.
   1957. Isaac Flood Arnow. Oriole 22(2):13-16.

Griscom, L.
   1923. Descriptions of apparently new birds from
   North America and the West Indies. Am. Mus.
   Novit. 71:1-8.

Griscom, L.
   1945. Modern bird study. 190 p. Harvard Univ.
   Press, Cambridge, Mass.

Griscom, L.
   1948. The changing seasons: a summary of the spring
   migration. Audubon Field Notes 2:167-168.

Griscom, L.
   1951. The changing seasons: a summary of the spring
   migration. Audubon Field Notes 5:243-244.

Griscom, L.
   1952. The changing seasons: a summary of the spring
   migration. Audubon Field Notes 6:235-236.

Griscom, L.
   1954. The changing seasons: a summary of the spring
   migration. Audubon Field Notes 8:296-297.

Griscom, L., and A. Sprunt, Jr., eds.
  1979. The warblers of America. Rev. and updated by
    E. M. Reilly, Jr. 302 p. Doubleday & Co., Gar-
    den City, N. Y.

Grosvenor, M. B., and A. Wetmore, eds.
  1937. The book of birds. vol. 2. 374 p. Natl.
    Geogr. Soc., Washington, D. C.

Gruson, E. S.
  1972. Words for birds. 305 p. Quadrangle Books,
    N. Y.

Gruson, E. S.
  1976. Checklist of the world's birds. 212 p.
    Quadrangle Books, N. Y.

Gundlach, J.
  1855. Beitrage zur ornithologie Cuba's. J. f.
    Ornithol. 3:465-480.

Gundlach, J.
  1861a. Beitrage zur ornithologie Cuba's. J. f.
    Ornithol. 9:401-416.

Gundlach, J.
  1861b. Tabellarische uebersicht aller bisher auf
    Cuba beobachteten vogel. J. f. Ornithol.
    9:321-349.

Gundlach, J.
  1865. Revista y catalogo de las aves Cubanas.
    Repert. Fisico. Nat. Cuba 1:221-242.

Gundlach, J.
  1876. Contribucion a la ornitologia Cubana. 364 p.
    "La Antilla", Habana.

Gundlach, J.
  1893. Ornitologia Cubana. 32 p. La Moderna,
    Habana.

Gunter, A. Y.
  1972. Big Thicket: A challenge for conservation.
    Jenkins Publ. Co., Austin, Texas. [Not seen,
    fide Oberholser 1974.]

Hader, R. J.
  1969. Species list of birds of Wake County, North
    Carolina. Chat 33(3):53-71.

Hamel, P. B.
    1976.   Searches for Bachman's Warblers in I'On
    Swamp, South Carolina.   Unpublished report.   24 p.
    USDA For. Serv., Southeast. For. Exp. Stn., Clem-
    son, S. C. [On file at R. M. Cooper Libr., Clem-
    son Univ., Clemson, S. C.] SEE: Harrison et al.
    1977.

Hamel, P. B.
    1977a. Final report to the Charleston Natural His-
    tory Society for an E. B. Chamberlain research
    grant entitled "Behavior and ecology of Bachman's
    Warbler in South Carolina." 3 p. [On file at R.
    M. Cooper Libr., Clemson Univ., Clemson, S. C.]

Hamel, P. B.
    1977b. Final report to the National Audubon Society
    for "A field study to determine the status of
    Bachman's Warbler on the Francis Beidler Memorial
    Forest, South Carolina." 8 p. [On file at R. M.
    Cooper Libr., Clemson Univ., Clemson, S. C.] SEE:
    Harrison et al. 1977.

Hamel, P. B.
    1977c. Problem analysis: research to determine the
    status of Bachman's Warbler, and the evolutionary,
    ecological, and historical factors associated with
    its decline. USDA For. Serv. Problem Analysis
    FS-SE-1702-1(76), 25 p. Southeast. For. Exp.
    Stn., Clemson, S. C. [On file at R. M. Cooper
    Libr., Clemson Univ., Clemson, S. C.]

Hamel, P. B.
    1977d. A list of the known nests of Bachman's War-
    bler. Unpubl. manuscript. 3 p. [On file at R.
    M. Cooper Libr., Clemson Univ., Clemson, S. C.]
    SEE: Shuler 1977g.

Hamel, P. B.
    1978.   Report on an attempt to develop an evolution-
    ary hypothesis for the family Parulidae. Unpub-
    lished report. 12 p. Southeast. For. Exp. Stn.,
    Clemson, S. C. [On file at R. M. Cooper Libr.,
    Clemson Univ., Clemson, S. C.]

Hamel, P. B.
    1979.   Bachman's Warbler: The decline (and fall?)
    of an endangered species. ABSTRACT. Amer. Zool.
    19:1003.

Hamel, P. B.
    1980.   Guidelines for management of wood warblers
    (Parulidae) on the Francis Marion National Forest.
    55 p.   Unpublished report.   USDA Forest Serv.,
    Columbia, S. C. [On file at R.   M. Cooper Libr.,
    Clemson Univ., Clemson, S. C.]

Hamel, P. B.
    1981.   A hierarchical approach to avian community
    structure.   323 p.   Ph. D. Diss., Dept. of Zool-
    ogy, Clemson Univ.   [Abstract in Diss. Abstr.
    Int. 43(2):331. 1982.]

Hamel, P. B.
    1984.   Bird - habitat relationships on southern for-
    est lands.   U. S.   Dep. Agric., Forest Serv.,
    Southern Region, Atlanta, Ga., in press.

Hamel, P. B., and S. A. Gauthreaux, Jr.
    1982.   The field identification of Bachman's Warbler
    (*Vermivora bachmanii* Audubon).   Amer. Birds
    36(3):235-240.

Hamel, P. B., and R. G. Hooper
    1979a.   The status of Bachman's Warbler, a progress
    report.   Proc.   Rare and Endangered Wildl. Symp.,
    Athens, Ga.:112-121.

Hamel, P. B., and R. G. Hooper
    1979b.   Bachman's Warbler -- the most critically
    endangered.   Proc.   S. C. Endangered Species Symp.
    1976:164-168.

Hamel, P. B., R. G. Hooper, D. F. Urbston, and A. McDo-
    nald
    1977.   Bachman's Warbler breeding habitat - a
    hypothesis.   Presented to 95th stated meeting, Am.
    Ornithol. Union, Berkeley, Ca.   [On file at R. M.
    Cooper Libr., Clemson Univ., Clemson, S. C.]

Hamel, P. B., R. G. Hooper, and L. M. Wright
    1976.   Where is the Reverend Bachman's Warbler?   S.
    C. Wildlife 23(2):9-13.

Hamel, P. B., H. E. LeGrand, Jr., M. R. Lennartz, and
    S. A.   Gauthreaux, Jr.
    1982.   Bird - habitat relationships on southeastern
    forest lands.   U.   S. Dep. Agric. Forest Serv.,
    Gen. Tech. Rep. SE-22.   417 p.   Southeastern For.
    Exp. Stn., Asheville, N. C.

65

Hanes, J. W.
   1958. Some notes on a Bachman's Warbler and his
   song. Atlantic Nat. 13(4):233-235.

Harrison, C.
   1978. A field guide to the nests, eggs, and nes-
   tlings of North American birds. 416 p. Collins,
   Glasgow.

Harrison, H. H.
   1948. American birds in color: land birds. 486 p.
   W. H. Wise, N. Y.

Harrison, J. R.
   1974. Preliminary bibliography of Bachman's Warbler. Unpublished manuscript. 6 p. [On file at
   R. M. Cooper Libr., Clemson Univ., Clemson, S. C.]

Harrison, J. R., W. C. Blakeney, W. D. Chamberlain, P.
   B. Laurie, and P. E. Nugent
   1977. Report of the ad hoc committee on Bachman's
   Warbler to the executive committee of the Charles-
   ton Natural History Society. 12 p. [On file at
   R. M. Cooper Libr., Clemson Univ, Clemson, S. C.]
   SEE: Evenden et al. 1976a, Hamel 1976, Hamel
   1977b.

Hausman, L. A.
   1944. The illustrated encyclopedia of American
   birds. 541 p. Halcyon House, N. Y.

Hausman, L. A.
   1946. Fieldbook of eastern birds. 658 p. G. P.
   Putnam's Sons, N. Y.

Headstrom, R.
   1949. Birds' nests: a field guide. 128 p. Ives
   Washburn, N. Y.

Hellmayr, C. E.
   1935. Catalogue of birds of the Americas, and the
   adjacent islands, part 8. Field Mus. Nat. Hist.
   Publ. 347, Zool. Ser., vol. 13. 541 p.

Hirsch, W.
   1973. [Anodized aluminum sculpture of Bachman's
   Warbler.] Alumni Music Center, Newberry Coll.,
   Newberry, S. C. SEE: Page 109 of this bibliography.

Holmes, R. P.
    1977. CBC Roundtable: comment on identification of
    Bachman's Warblers. Chat 41(2):28-29.

Holt, E. G.
    1920. Bachman's Warbler breeding in Alabama. Auk
    37:103-104.

Hooper, R. G., and P. B. Hamel
    1974. Study plan for a cooperative study to deter-
    mine the status of Bachman's Warbler on the Fran-
    cis Marion National Forest in South Carolina.
    USDA For. Serv. Study Plan FS-SE-1951-1, 25 p.
    Southeast. For. Exp. Stn., Clemson, S. C. [On
    file at R. M. Cooper Libr., Clemson Univ., Clem-
    son, S. C.]

Hooper, R. G., and P. B. Hamel
    1977. Nesting habitat of Bachman's Warbler -- a
    review. Wilson Bull. 89(3):373-379. SEE: Shu-
    ler 1977h.

Hooper, R. G., and P. B. Hamel
    1979. Status of Swainson's Warbler in South Caro-
    lina. Proc. S. C. Endangered Species Symp.
    1976:178-182.

Horlbeck, E. M.
    1958. Spider's web leads to an ornithological
    discovery. Audubon 60:214-215.

Howe, M. A.
    1978. The changing seasons. Amer. Birds
    32:968-976.

Howell, A. H.
    1910. Notes on the birds of the sunken lands of
    southeastern Missouri. Auk 27:381-384.

Howell, A. H.
    1911. Birds of Arkansas. USDA Bur. Biol. Surv.
    Bull. 38, 100 p.

Howell, A. H.
    1928. Birds of Alabama, 2nd ed. 384 p. Dep. Game
    and Fisheries of Ala., Montgomery.

Howell, A. H.
    1932. Florida bird life. 579 p. Fla. Dep. Game
    and Freshwater Fish, Tallahassee.

Hoxie, W. J.
   1911. Birds of Chatham County, Georgia. Savannah
   News, 8 installments beginning 30 April 1911.

Imhof, T. A.
   1962. Alabama birds. 591 p. Univ. Ala. Press,
   Birmingham.

Imhof, T. A.
   1966. Central southern region. Audubon Field Notes
   20:515-519.

Imhof, T. A.
   1973. Central southern region. Am. Birds
   27:782-785.

Imhof, T. A.
   1976. Alabama birds, 2nd ed. 445 p. Ala. Univ.
   Press, University, Ala.

Imhof, T. A.
   1977. Central southern region. Am. Birds
   31(5):1010-1013.

James, D. J. and J. C. Neal.
   1987. Arkansas Birds--Their distribution and
   abundance. in press. Univ. of Arkansas Press,
   Fayetteville.

Johnson, A. S., and L. L. Landers.
   1982. Habitat relationships of summer resident
   birds in slash pine flatwoods. Journ. Wildl. Manage. 46(2):416-428.

Johnston, D. W.
   1962. The 1962 spring count. Chat 26(3):58-69.

Jones, L.
   1900. Warbler songs (Mniotiltidae). Wilson Bull.
   12(1):1-57.

Keast, A.
   1980. Spatial relationships between migratory Paru-
   lid warblers and their ecological counterparts in
   the Neotropics. In Migrant birds in the Neotropics: Ecology, behavior, distribution, and conservation. p. 109-130. A. Keast and E. S. Morton,
   eds. Smithsonian Inst. Press, Washington, D. C.

Keeler, J.
    1976. Birds. In Endangered and Threatened Plants
    and Animals of Alabama. p.80-87. H. Boschung,
    ed. Bull. Ala. Mus. Nat. Hist., 2.

Keller, C. E., S. A. Keller, and T. C. Keller
    1979. Indiana birds and their haunts. 214 p.
    Indiana Univ. Press, Bloomington.

King, W. B.
    1978. Survival Service Commission red data book.
    vol. 2. Aves. 2nd rev. ed. Looseleaf. Inter-
    nat. Union for Conserv. of Nature and Nat.
    Resources, Morges, Switzerland.

Kleen, V., and L. Bush
    1971. A field list of the birds of southern Illi-
    nois. 20 p. Southern Illinois Univ., Carbondale.

Klimkiewicz, M. K., and C. S. Robbins
    1978. Standard abbreviations for common names of
    birds. No. Amer. Bird Bander 3(1):16-25.

Kopman, H. H.
    1905. Warbler migration in southeast Louisiana and
    southern Mississippi. Auk 22:289-296.

Kopman, H. H.
    1915. List of the birds of Louisiana. Part 7. Auk
    32:183-194.

Korte, P. A., and L. H. Fredrickson
    1977. Loss of Missouri's lowland hardwood ecosys-
    tem. Trans. N. A. Wildl. and Nat. Res. Conf.
    42:31-41.

Lane, J. A.
    1981. A birder's guide to Florida. 160 p. L & P
    Press, Denver, Colorado.

LaPrade, W. H., Jr.
    1922. Breeding warblers around Atlanta, Georgia.
    Wilson Bull. 34:80-83.

Larner, Y. R., and Checklist Committee of the Virginia
    Society of Ornithologists
    1979. Virginia's birdlife: an annotated checklist.
    Va. Soc. Ornithol., Va. Avifauna No. 2, 118 p.

Lawrence, G. N.
   1887a. The rediscovery of Bachman's Warbler *Helminthophila bachmani* (Aud.), in the United States. Auk
   4:35-37.

Lawrence, G. N.
   1887b. Additional specimens of Bachman's and Swainson's Warblers, obtained by Mr. Chas. S. Galbraith, in the spring of 1887. Auk 4:262-263.

Laycock, G.
   1969. America's endangered wildlife. 226 p. Gros-
   set & Dunlap, N. Y.

LeGrand, H. E., Jr.
   1975. Distribution and abundance of the wood warblers in North Carolina during the spring, nesting, and fall seasons. Chat 39:45-54.

LeGrand, H. E., Jr.
   1979. Southern Atlantic coast region. Amer. Birds
   33:760-762.

LeGrand, H. E., Jr., and P. B. Hamel
   1980. Bird - habitat associations on southeastern
   forest lands. 276 p. Report submitted to Southeast. For. Exp. Stn., Clem- son, S. C. [On file
   at R. M. Cooper Libr., Clemson Univ., Clemson, S.
   C.]

Lembeye, J.
   1850. Aves de la isla de Cuba. 139 p. Imprenta
   del Tiempo, Habana.

Lesser Squawk
   1958a. The rarest of warblers. Lesser Squawk
   6(1):3.

Lesser Squawk
   1958b. [Bachman's Warbler.] Lesser Squawk 6(2):1.

Lesser Squawk
   1958c. Bachman's Warbler again. Lesser Squawk
   6(3):1.

Lesser Squawk
   1959. Bachman's Warbler. Lesser Squawk 10(2):1.

Lesser Squawk
   1960. More on Bachman's Warbler. Lesser Squawk
      8(1):2.

Lesser Squawk
   1961a. Spring bird count. Lesser Squawk 9(1):3.

Lesser Squawk
   1961b. Arrival dates of summer residents and spring
      transients. Lesser Squawk 9(2):3-4.

Lesser Squawk
   1962. Observations. Lesser Squawk 9(12):4.

Lesser Squawk
   1969. Observations. Lesser Squawk 20(12):2.

Lesser Squawk
   1973. Observations. Lesser Squawk 24(9):6.

Lowery, G. H., Jr.
   1974. Louisiana birds, 3rd ed. 651 p. La. State
      Univ. Press, Baton Rouge, La.

Lowery, G. H., Jr., and B. L. Monroe, Jr.
   1968. Parulidae. In Checklist of birds of the
      world. vol. 14. p. 3-93. R. A. Paynter, Jr.,
      ed. Mus. Comp. Zool., Cambridge, Mass.

Lowery, G. H., Jr., and R. J. Newman
   1952. Central southern region. Audubon Field Notes
      6:249-252.

McClung, R. M.
   1969. Lost wild America. 240 p. W. Morrow, N. Y.

Mackenzie, J. P. S.
   1977. Birds in peril. 191 p. Houghton-Mifflin
      Co., Boston.

Mayfield, H.
   1950. Middlewestern prairie region. Audubon Field
      Notes 4:243-245.

Maynard, C. J.
   1890. Eggs of North American birds. 159 p.
      DeWolfe, Fiske and Co., Boston.

Maynard, C. J.
    1889-1896. Birds of eastern North America, rev. ed.
    721 p. C. J. Maynard, Newtonville, Mass.

Mayr, E., and L. L. Short
    1970. Species taxa of North American birds. Publ.
    Nutt. Ornithol. Club, 9, 127 p.

Meanley, B.
    1951. Bachman's Warbler - our rarest passerine
    bird. Atlantic Nat. 6:10-13.

Meanley, B.
    1971. Natural history of the Swainson's Warbler.
    USDI Bur. Sport Fish. and Wildl., North Amer.
    Fauna, 69, 90 p.

Meanley, B.
    1972. Swamps, river bottoms, and canebrakes. 142
    p. Barre Publ., Barre, Mass.

Meanley, B.
    1975. Birds and marshes of the Chesapeake Bay coun-
    try. 157 p. Tidewater Publ., Cambridge, Md.

Meanley, B., and R. T. Mitchell
    1958. Food habits of Bachman's Warbler. Atlantic
    Nat. 13(4):236-238.

Mengel, R. M.
    1948. Some records of importance to Kentucky orni-
    thology. Ky. Warbler 24(4):49-54.

Mengel, R. M.
    1964. The probable history of species formation in
    some northern Wood Warblers (Parulidae). Living
    Bird 3:9-44.

Mengel, R. M.
    1965. The birds of Kentucky. Am. Ornithol. Union,
    Monogr. 3, 581 p.

Merriam, C. H.
    1887. Another specimen of Bachman's Warbler (*Helmin-
    thophila bachmani*). Auk 4:262.

Morony, J. J., Jr., W. J. Bock, and J. Farrand, Jr.
    1975. Reference list of the birds of the world.
    207 p. Am. Mus. Nat. Hist., N. Y.

Mumford, R. E., and C. E. Keller
   1975.   An annotated checklist of Indiana birds.
   Indiana Audubon Q.   53(2):28-63.

Murphy, R. C., and D. Amadon
   1953.   Land birds of America.   240 p.   McGraw-Hill,
   N. Y.

Murray, J. J.
   1933.   Additions to the Virginia avifauna since
   1890.   Auk 50:190-200.

Murray, J. J.
   1952.   A checklist of the birds of Virginia.   113 p.
   Va. Soc. of Ornithol.

National Wildl. Fed.
   1976.   On the legal front.   Rep. to Natl. Wildl.
   Fed. Members August-Sept., 1976.

Nehrling, H.
   1906.   Bird-life in my Florida garden during the
   months of September and October.   Warbler (ser.
   2)2:11-19.

Newman, R. J.
   1954.   Central southern region.   Audubon Field Notes
   8:316-319.

Newman, R. J.
   1955.   Central southern region.   Audubon Field Notes
   9:335-338.

Newman, R. J.
   1958.   Central southern region.   Audubon Field Notes
   12:358-362.

Newman, R. J., and S. L. Warter
   1959a. Central southern region.   Audubon Field Notes
   13:376-380.

Newman, R. J., and S. L. Warter
   1959b. Central southern region.   Audubon Field Notes
   13:434-437.

New Yorker
   1950.   Rare bird.   New Yorker 26(29):26.

Northwood, J. d'A.
   1956.   Audubon's firsts.   Atlantic Nat.
   11(5):222-229.

Nugent, P. E.
  1976. South Carolina birds: a check list, rev. ed.
  Charleston Nat. Hist. Soc., Charleston, S. C.

Oberholser, H. C.
  1905. Notes on the nomenclature of certain genera
  of birds. Smithson. Misc. Coll. 48:59-68.

Oberholser, H. C.
  1938. Bird life of Louisiana. La. Dep. Conserv.
  Bull. 28, 834 p. New Orleans.

Oberholser, H. C.
  1974. The bird life of Texas. vol. 2. p.
  531-1069. Univ. Tex. Press, Austin, Tex.

Odom, R.
  1976. Endangered wildlife. Outdoors in Ga.
  5:22-26.

Olendorff, R. R., and W. D. Zeedyk
  1978. Land management for the conservation of
  endangered birds. In Endangered Birds: Proc.
  symp. management techniques for preserving threatened species, 1977. p. 419-428. S. A. Temple,
  ed. Univ. Wisconsin Pr., Madison, Wisc.

Ostroff, S. J.
  1985. A phenetic study of the wood warblers
  (Parulinae). Ph. D. diss. University of Toronto,
  Toronto, Ontario, Canada.

Palmer, W.
  1894. Four additions to the birds of the Virginias.
  Auk 11:333-334.

Parnell, J. F., J. H. Carter, III, D. S. Lee, E. F.
  Potter, and R. P. Teulings
  1978. Checklist of North Carolina birds. 37 p.
  Carolina Bird Club and N. C. State Mus. Nat.
  Hist., Raleigh, N. C.

Pasquier, R. F.
  1977. Watching birds. 301 p. Houghton-Mifflin,
  Boston.

Paterson, A.
  1972. Birds of the Bahamas. 180 p. Durrell Publ.,
  Brattleboro, Vt.

Pearson, T. G., C. S. Brimley, and H. H. Brimley
   1942. Birds of North Carolina. 416 p. N. C. Dep.
   Agric., Raleigh.

Peterson, R. T.
   1947. A field guide to the birds, 2nd rev. ed. 290
   p. Houghton Mifflin, Boston.

Peterson, R. T.
   1948. Birds over America. 342 p. Dodd, Mead, and
   Co., N. Y.

Peterson, R. T.
   1963. A field guide to the birds of Texas and adjacent states. 304 p. Houghton Mifflin, Boston.

Peterson, R. T.
   1980. A field guide to the birds, 4th ed. 384 p.
   Houghton Mifflin, Boston.

Pettingill, O. S., Jr.
   1951. A guide to bird finding east of the Mississippi. 659 p. Oxford Univ. Press, N. Y.

Pettingill, O. S., Jr.
   1970. Ornithology in laboratory and field, 4th ed.
   524 p. Burgess Publ. Co., Minneapolis.

Pindar, L. O.
   1923. Bachman's Warbler at Versailles, Kentucky.
   Wilson Bull. 35(2):115. SEE: Mengel 1965.

Potter, E. F., J. F. Parnell, and R. P. Teulings
   1980. Birds of the Carolinas. 408 p. Univ. N. C.
   Press, Chapel Hill, N. C.

Potter, J. K., and J. J. Murray
   1954. Middle Atlantic Coast region. Audubon Field
   Notes 8:303-305.

Pough, R. H.
   1946. Audubon bird guide: eastern land birds. 312
   p. Doubleday, Garden City, N. Y.

Rappole, J. H., E. S. Morton, T. E. Lovejoy, III, J. L.
   Ruos, and B. Swift.
   1983. Nearctic avian migrants in the neotropics.
   646 p. U. S. Dept. Interior, Fish and Wildlife
   Service, Washington, D. C.

Rea, P. M.
   1909. Report of the director of the museum for the
   year 1908. Bull. Charleston Mus. 5(1):1-11.

Rea, P. M., and F. M. Weston, Jr.
   1909. Preliminary survey of the birds of the coast
   region of South Carolina. Bull. Charleston Mus.
   5:13-24, 27-32.

Read, A. C.
   1909a. From the Isle of Pines. Oologist 26:57-58.

Read, A. C.
   1909b. Birds on the Isle of Pines. Forest & Stream
   73:452.

Read, A. C.
   1911. List of birds observed by A. C. Read on the
   Isle of Pines, Cuba, from December, 1908, to
   December, 1909. Oologist 28:11-13.

Read, A. C.
   1913. Birds observed on the Isle of Pines from
   December, 1908, to January, 1912, which were not
   seen during 1912 by A. C. Read. The dates are
   first records. Oologist 30:131.

Reed [Read], A. C.
   1911. Birds seen on one ten acre tract in West
   McKinley, Isle of Pines, Cuba. Oologist
   28:113-114.

Reed, C. A.
   1965. North American birds eggs. 372 p. Dover
   Publ., N. Y. [Reprint of 1904 ed. published by
   Doubleday, Page, and Co.]

Rehn, J. A. G.
   1905. Bachman's Warbler in Leon County, Florida.
   Auk 22:85.

Reilly, E. M., Jr.
   1954. Bird records and the A. O. U. Check-list
   ranges. Auk 71:156-163.

Reilly, E. M., Jr.
   1968. The Audubon illustrated handbook of American
   birds. 524 p. McGraw-Hill, N. Y.

Remsen, J. V., Jr.
   1986. Was Bachman's Warbler a bamboo specialist?
   Auk 103(1):216-219.

Richardson, J.
    1837. Report on North American zoology. Rep. Brit.
    Assoc. Advancement of Sci. 1836:121-224.

Ridgway, R.
    1874. Catalogue of the birds ascertained to occur
    in Illinois. Ann. Lyceum Nat. Hist., N. Y.
    10:364-394.

Ridgway, R.
    1876. Notes on the genus *Helminthophaga*. Ibis
    6:166-171.

Ridgway, R.
    1878. Notes on birds observed at Mount Carmel,
    southern Illinois, in the spring of 1878. Bull.
    Nutt. Ornithol. Club 3(4):162-166. SEE: Gault
    1922, Ridgway 1881c, Smith and Parmalee 1955.

Ridgway, R.
    1881a. Nomenclature of North American birds,
    chiefly contained in the U. S. National Museum.
    U. S. Nat. Mus. Bull. 21, 94 p.

Ridgway, R.
    1881b. Catalogue of the birds of North America.
    Proc. U. S. Nat. Mus. 3:163-246.

Ridgway, R.
    1881c. A catalogue of the birds of Illinois. Ill.
    State Lab. Nat. Hist. Bull. 4:163-208.

Ridgway, R.
    1882. On the generic name *Helminthophaga*. Bull.
    Nutt. Ornithol. Club 7:53-54.

Ridgway, R.
    1887. Manual of North American birds. 631 p. Lip-
    pincott, Phila.

Ridgway, R.
    1889. The ornithology of Illinois. part I.
    Descriptive catalog. vol. 1. 520 p. State Lab.
    Nat. Hist., Springfield, Ill.

Ridgway, R.
    1896. Manual of North American birds, 2nd ed. 653
    p. Lippincott, Phila.

Ridgway, R.
    1897. Description of the nest and eggs of Bachman's
    Warbler (*Helminthophila bachmanii*). Auk 14:309-310.

Ridgway, R.
    1902.   The birds of North and Middle America.   Pt.
    2.   Tanagridae - Mniotiltidae.   U. S. Nat. Mus.
    Bull. 50, 834 p.

Riley, J. H.
    1905.   Birds of the Bahama Islands.   In The Bahama
    Islands.   p. 347-368.   G. B. Shattuck, ed.   Mac-
    Millan, N. Y.

Riley, L., and W. Riley
    1979.   Guide to the National Wildlife Refuges.   653
    p. Doubleday, Garden City, N. Y.

Ripley, S. D., and A. Moreno
    1980.   A recent sighting of Bachman's Warbler in
    Cuba.   Birding 12:211-212.

Roads, K. M.
    1912.   Why birds are so named, 2.   Wilson Bull.
    24:27-33, 130-142.

Robbins, C. S.
    1950.   The changing seasons: a summary of the spring
    migration.   Audubon Field Notes 4:231-233.

Robbins, C. S., B. Bruun, H. S. Zim, and A. Singer
    1966.   Birds of North America.   340 p.   Golden
    Press, N. Y.

Robbins, C. S., W. Harrison, G. S. Keith, R. G. McCa-
    skie, R. T.   Peterson, N. Pettingell, O. S. Pet-
    tingill, Jr., A. Small, R. W. Smart, and J. A.
    Tucker
    1975.   A. B. A. Checklist: Birds of continental
    United States and Canada.   64 p.   Amer. Birding
    Assn., Austin, Texas.

Robbins, P.
    1975.   "A wonderfully hospitable place."   S. C.
    Wildlife 22(2):9-15.

Robertson, W.
    1962.   Appendix: Specific area Report: proposed
    Congaree Swamp National Monument.   11 p.   USDI
    Nat. Park Serv., Richmond, Va.

Robinson, W. L., and E. G. Bolen.
    1984.   Wildlife ecology and management.   478 p.
    MacMillan, N. Y.

Ruch, B. H.
    1954. May regional census. Atlantic Nat. 10:33-37.

Saunders, A. A.
    1908. Some birds of central Alabama. Auk
    25:413-424.

Saunders, A. A.
    1951. A guide to bird songs, rev. ed. 307 p.
    Doubleday, Garden City, N. Y.

Sciple, G. W.
    1950. Recent record of Bachman's Warbler, *Vermivora
    bachmanii*, from Gulf Coast of Mississippi. Auk
    67:520.

Scott, S. L., ed.
    1983. Field guide to the birds of North America.
    464 p. National Geographic Society, Washington,
    D. C.

Scott, W. E. D.
    1887. Another Bachman's Warbler in Florida. Auk
    4:348.

Scott, W. E. D.
    1888a. Supplementary notes from the Gulf Coast of
    Florida, with a description of a new species of
    Marsh Wren. Auk 5:183-188.

Scott, W. E. D.
    1888b. Bachman's Warbler (*Helminthophila bachmani*) at
    Key West, Florida in July and August. Auk
    5:428-430.

Scott, W. E. D.
    1890a. A summary of observations on the birds of the
    Gulf Coast of Florida. Auk 7:14-22.

Scott, W. E. D.
    1890b. On birds observed at the Dry Tortugas, Flo-
    rida, during parts of March and April, 1890. Auk
    7:301-314.

Scott, W. E. D.
    1892. Notes on the birds of the Caloosahatchie
    region of Florida. Auk 9(3):209-218.

Sharpe, R. B.
    1885. Catalogue of the Passeriformes, or perching
    birds, in the collection of the British Museum.
    vol. 10. Fringilliformes. Pt. I. Dicaeidae,
    Hirundinidae, Ampelidae, Mniotiltidae, and Mota-
    cillidae. 682 p. Taylor and Francis, London.

Short, E. H.
    1905. Bachman's Warbler. Oologist 22:103.

Short, L. L.
    1981. Birds. In Harper & Row's complete field
    guide to North American wildlife. p. 1-220. H.
    H. Collins, ed. Harper & Row, Publ., New York.

Shugart, H. H., T. M. Smith, J. T. Kitchings, and R. L.
    Kroodsma
    1978. The relationship of nongame birds to southern
    forest types and successional stages. In Proceed.
    workshop. management of southern forests for non-
    game birds. p. 5-16. R. M. DeGraaf, Tech. Coord.
    USDA For. Serv., Gen. Tech. Rep. SE-14. South-
    east. For. Exp. Stn., Asheville, N. C.

Shuler, J.
    1976. Bachman's Warbler and its South Carolina
    habitat. 31 p. Unpublished manuscript. [On file
    at R. M. Cooper Libr., Clemson Univ., Clemson, S.
    C.]

Shuler, J.
    1977a. Three recent sight records of Bachman's War-
    bler. Chat 41(1):11-12.

Shuler, J.
    1977b. Bachman's Warbler habitat. Chat 41(2):19-23.
    SEE: Shuler 1977e is a reprint of this work.

Shuler, J.
    1977c. CBC Roundtable: further comment on the vari-
    able Bachman's Warbler. Chat 41(2):29.

Shuler, J.
    1977d. Bachman's phantom warbler. Birding
    9(6):245-250.

Shuler, J.
    1977e. Bachman's Warbler habitat. Birding
    9(6):251-254. SEE: This is reprint of Shuler
    1977b.

Shuler, J.
   1977f. Bachman's Warbler in a clear-cut? Lesser
      Squawk 28(11):7-8.

Shuler, J.
   1977g. Critique of "Nesting habitat of Bachman's
      Warbler - a review." Unpublished manuscript. 6
      p. [On file at R. M. Cooper Libr., Clemson Univ.,
      Clemson, S. C.] SEE: Hooper and Hamel 1977a.

Shuler, J.
   1978. Red Crossbill in June near Charleston, S. C.
      Chat 42(1):14.

Shuler, J.
   1979a. Clutch size and onset of laying in Bachman's
      Warbler. Chat 43:27-29. SEE: Hamel 1977d.

Shuler, J.
   1979b. Subsequent note. Birding 11:274. SEE:
      Bass 1979a.

Shuler, J.
   1979c. Clutch size and onset of laying in Bachman's
      Warbler. Birding 11:275-278. SEE: This is a
      reprint of Shuler 1979a.

Shuler, J.
   1979d. The boy who wanted to paint birds. Birding
      11:280-283.

Shuler, J., P. Nugent, J. Trochet, and J. Van Os
   1978. Bachman's Warbler observations continue in
      I'On Swamp. Chat 42(2):23-24.

Shuler, J., P. Nugent, J. Trochet, and J. Van Os
   1979. Observations in I'On Swamp in 1977. Birding
      11:268-270. SEE: This is a reprint of Shuler et
      al. 1978.

Shuler, J., and A. E. Sanders
   1977. A new look at the type locality of the Bach-
      man's Warbler. Chat 41(1):12-13.

Smith, A. P.
   1915. Birds of the Boston Mountains, Arkansas.
      Condor 17:41-57.

Smith, E. T.
    1941. Chicago region. Audubon 41(4, sect.
    2):392-393.

Smith, H. R., and P. W. Parmalee
    1955. A distributional checklist of the birds of
    Illinois. Ill. State Mus. Pop. Sci. Ser. 4:1-62.

Sprunt, A., Jr.
    1931. In memoriam: Arthur T. Wayne. Auk 48:1-16.

Sprunt, A., Jr.
    1954a. Florida bird life. 527 p. Coward-McCann, N.
    Y.

Sprunt, A., Jr.
    1954b. Unpredictable Bachman's Warbler. Audubon
    56:172-173, 179.

Sprunt, A., Jr.
    1958. The rare Bachman's Warbler again. Audubon
    60:214.

Sprunt, A., Jr.
    1963. Addendum to Florida bird-life [sic]. 24 p.
    mimeo. [publisher unlisted], Charleston, S. C.

Sprunt, A., Jr.
    1965. Bull's Island, S. C. In The bird watcher's
    America. p. 41-47. O. S. Pettingill, Jr., ed.
    McGraw-Hill, N. Y.

Sprunt, A., Jr., and E. B. Chamberlain
    1970. South Carolina bird life, rev. ed. [Reprint
    of 1949 ed. with a Supplement by E. M. Burton.]
    655 p. Univ. S. C. Press, Columbia.

Stansell, K. B.
    1976. Toward extinction. S. C. Wildlife
    23(6):45-49.

Stein, R. C.
    1968a. Correlations among song pattern, morphology,
    and distribution within the genus *Vermivora* (Paru-
    lidae). Biehefte der Vogelwelt 1:139-146.

Stein, R. C.
    1968b. Modulation in bird sounds. Auk
    85(2):229-243.

Stevens, O. A.
   1936. The first descriptions of North American
      birds. Wilson Bull. 48:203-215.

Stevenson, H. M.
   1938. Bachman's Warbler in Alabama. Wilson Bull.
      50:36-41.

Stevenson, H. M.
   1956. Florida region. Audubon Field Notes
      10:325-329. SEE: Stevenson 1958.

Stevenson, H. M.
   1957. The relative magnitude of the trans-Gulf and
      circum-Gulf spring migration. Wilson Bull.
      69:39-77.

Stevenson, H. M.
   1958. Florida region. Audubon Field Notes
      12:405-408. SEE: Stevenson, 1956.

Stevenson, H. M.
   1972a. Further comments on Bachman's Warbler (*Vermi-
      vora bachmanii*). Fla. Nat. 45(4):129.

Stevenson, H. M.
   1972b. The recent history of Bachman's Warbler.
      Wilson Bull. 84(3):344-347.

Stevenson, H. M.
   1975. Report on two searches for Bachman's Warbler.
      10 p. Unpublished report. USDA For. Serv.,
      Southeast. For. Exp. Stn., Clemson, S. C. [On
      file at R. M. Cooper Libr., Clemson Univ., Clem-
      son, S. C.]

Stevenson, H. M.
   1976. Vertebrates of Florida: identification and
      distribution. 607 p. Univ. Presses of Fla.,
      Gainesville, Fla.

Stevenson, H. M.
   1978. Endangered Bachman's Warbler. In Birds.
      vol. 2. p. 13-14. H. W. Kale, II, ed. In Rare
      and endangered biota of Florida. P. C. H. Pritch-
      ard, ed. Univ. Florida Press, Gainesville.

Stevenson, H. M.
   1982. Bachman's Warbler . . . rarest North American
      bird? Florida Wildl. March-April:36-39.

Stewart, D.
    1978. From the edge of extinction. 191 p.
    Methuen, N. Y.

Studer, J. H., ed.
    1888. The birds of North America. 192 p. Nat.
    Science Assn. of America, N. Y.

Sutton, G. M.
    1967. Oklahoma birds. 674 p. Univ. Okla. Press,
    Norman, Okla.

Swainson, W.
    1827. A synopsis of the birds discovered in Mexico
    by W. Bullock, F. L. S. and H. S., and Mr. William
    Bullock, Jr. Philos. Mag., Lond. n. s., I, June
    1827:433-442. [Although this paper antedates the
    discovery of Bachman's Warbler by five years, it
    is important for in it Swainson established *Vermi-
    vora* as a valid generic name within Parulidae.]

Tanner, J. T.
    1939. Observations in Madison Parish, Louisiana.
    Auk 56:90.

Taylor, J. W.
    1972. Bachman's Warbler, America's rarest songbird.
    Fla. Nat. 45(2):49-51, 67.

Terborgh, J.
    1974. Preservation of natural diversity: the prob-
    lem of extinction prone species. BioScience
    24(12):715-722.

Terborgh, J. W.
    1980. The conservation status of Neotropical mig-
    rants: Present and future. In Migrant birds in
    the Neotropics: Ecology, behavior, distribution,
    and conservation. p. 21-30. A. Keast and E. S.
    Morton, eds. Smithsonian Inst. Press, Washington,
    D. C.

Teulings, R. P.
    1978. Southern Atlantic coast region. Amer. Birds
    32:992-993.

Thayer, G. H.
    1906. A brief general classification of the songs
    of eastern wood warblers. Bird Lore 8:64-65.

Todd, W. E. C.
   1916.   The birds of the Isle of Pines.   Ann. Carne-
   gie Mus. 10:146-296.

Trotter, S.
   1887.   The significance of certain phases in the
   genus *Helminthophila*.   Auk 4:307-310.

Trudeau, G.
   1981.   Doonesbury.   Univ. Press Syndicate.   June.

True, F. W.
   1883.   Chapter 10.   A list of the vertebrate animals
   of South Carolina.   In South Carolina, Resources
   and population institutions and industries.   p.
   209-264.   State Board Agric., S. C.

[Tucker, J. A., ed.]
   1979.   Bachman's Warbler: ABA's most wanted bird.
   Birding 11:268.

USDA For. Serv.
   1969.   Protecting endangered wildlife on your southern National Forests.   21 p.   USDA For. Serv.
   South. Region, Atlanta.

USDA For. Serv.
   1977.   Francis Marion National Forest land management plan.   288 p.   USDA For. Serv. Southern
   Region, Atlanta, Ga.

USDA Forest Service, Southern Region.
   1985a.   Final environmental impact statement, Land
   resource management plan, Francis Marion National
   Forest, South Carolina.   604 p.   USDA Forest
   Service, Columbia, S. C.

USDA Forest Service, Southern Region.
   1985b.   Land and resource management plan, Francis
   Marion National Forest, South Carolina.   294 p.
   USDA Forest Service, Columbia, S. C.

USDI Fish and Wildl. Serv.
   1967.   Birds of the Cape Romain National Wildlife
   Refuge.   USDI Fish and Wildl. Serv. Refuge Leaflet
   101-R-4.

USDI Fish and Wildl. Serv.
   1971.   Accidental birds of the Okefenokee National
   Wildlife Refuge.   USDI Fish and Wildl. Serv. Refuge Leaflet 181A, 4 p.

USDI Fish and Wildl. Serv.
    1978.   Endangered and threatened species of the
    southeastern United States.   Looseleaf handbook.
    USDI Fish and Wildl. Serv., Atlanta, Ga.

USDI Fish and Wildl. Serv.
    1980.   Republication of lists of endangered and
    threatened species and correction of technical
    errors in final rules.   Federal Regist.
    45(99):33768-33781.

USDI Fish and Wildl. Serv., Nat. Fish and Wildl. Lab.
    1980.   Selected vertebrate endangered species of the
    seacoast of the United States - Bachman's Warbler.
    4 p.   Looseleaf.   USDI Fish and Wildl. Serv., Off.
    of Biol. Serv., Coastal Ecosys.   Proj., Slidell,
    La.

USDI Off. Endangered Species and Int. Activ.
    1973.   Threatened wildlife of the United States.
    USDI Fish. and Wildl.   Serv. Resour. Publ. 114,
    289 p.

Urbston, D., D. Mudge, and L. Lewis
    1979.   Historical aspects and ecosystem changes of
    Bachman's Warbler habitat in South Carolina.
    Proc. S. C. Endangered Species Symp.
    1976:169-177.

Vaughn, R. R.
    1978.   [Letter to L. Whitfield.]   18 p.   [This is
    the Biological Opinion rendered by the USDI Fish
    and Wildlife Service, Atlanta, GA, to the USDA
    Forest Service, Atlanta, GA, with respect to man-
    agement of National Forest lands in South Carolina
    for Bachman's Warblers.   Prepared by W. Parker.
    (On file at R. M. Cooper Libr., Clemson Univ.,
    Clemson, S. C.)]

Verner, J., and M. F. Willson
    1969.   Mating systems, sexual dimorphism, and the
    role of male North American passerine birds in the
    nesting cycle.   Am. Ornithol.   Union, Monogr. 9,
    76 p.

Vincent, J.
    1966. Survival Service Commission red data book.
    vol. 2. Aves. Looseleaf. Internat. Union for
    Conserv. of Nature and Nat. Resources, Morges,
    Switzerland.

Wallace, G. J., and H. D. Mahan
    1975. An introduction to ornithology, 3rd ed. 546
    p. MacMillan, N. Y

Wayne, A. S. [A. T.]
    1901. Bachman's Warbler (*Helminthophila bachmani*)
    rediscovered near Charleston, South Carolina. Auk
    18:274-275.

Wayne, A. T.
    1893. Additional notes on the birds of the Suwanee
    River. Auk 10:336-338.

Wayne, A. T.
    1895. Notes on the birds of the Wacissa and Aucilla
    River regions of Florida. Auk 12:362-367.

Wayne, A. T.
    1905. Notes on certain birds taken or seen near
    Charleston, South Carolina. Auk 22:395-400.

Wayne, A. T.
    1906. The date of discovery of Swainson's Warbler
    (*Helinaia swainsonii*). Auk 23:227.

Wayne, A. T.
    1907a. The nest and eggs of Bachman's Warbler, *Hel-
    minthophila bachmani* (Aud.), taken near Charleston,
    South Carolina. Auk 24:43-48.

Wayne, A. T.
    1907b. Observations on some birds procured near
    Charleston, South Carolina. Auk 24:377-382.

Wayne, A. T.
    1910a. Birds of South Carolina. Contrib. Charleston
    Mus. 1, 254 p.

Wayne, A. T.
    1910b. Concerning three erroneous Georgia records.
    Auk 27:213-214.

Wayne, A. T.
    1912. Bachman's Warbler in Camden Co. and breeding
    in Chatham Co., Georgia. Auk 29:105.

Wayne, A. T.
    1917. A list of avian species for which the type
    locality is South Carolina. Contrib. Charleston
    Mus. 3:1-8.

Wayne, A. T.
    1918. Some additions and other records new to the
    ornithology of South Carolina. Auk 35:437-442.

Wayne, A. T.
    1925. A late autumnal record for the Bachman's War-
    bler (*Vermivora bachmani*). Wilson Bull. 37:41.

Weston, F. M.
    1965. A survey of the birdlife of northwestern
    Florida. Bull. Tall Timbers Res. Stn. 5:1-147.

Wheeler, H. E.
    1924. The birds of Arkansas. 184 p. Arkansas Bur.
    Mines, Manufactures and Agric., Little Rock.

Widmann, O.
    1896. Bachman's Warbler (*Helminthophila bachmani*) in
    Greene County, Arkansas. Auk 13:264.

Widmann, O.
    1897. The summer home of Bachman's Warbler no
    longer unknown. Auk 14:305-309.

Widmann, O.
    1898. Bachman's Warbler in summer. Osprey 3:13.
    SEE: Short 1905.

Widmann, O.
    1907. A preliminary catalog of the birds of Mis-
    souri. Trans. Acad. Sci., St. Louis 17(1):1-288.

Wilcove, D. S., and J. W. Terborgh.
    1984. Patterns of population decline in birds.
    American Birds 38:10-13.

Williams, G. G.
    1945. Do birds cross the Gulf of Mexico in spring?
    Auk 62:98-111.

Williams, G. G.
   1950. The nature and causes of the 'coastal hia-
   tus'. Wilson Bull. 62(4):175-182.

Williams, R. W., Jr.
   1904. A preliminary list of the birds of Leon
   County, Florida. Auk 21:449-462.

Williams, R. W., Jr.
   1907. Additional notes on the birds of Leon County,
   Florida. Auk 24:158-159.

Wilson, E. S.
   1918. Bachman's Warbler and Solitary Sandpiper in
   Indiana. Auk 35:228-229. SEE: Mumford and
   Keller 1975.

Wilson, G.
   1922. Birds of Bowling Green, Kentucky. Auk
   39(2):233-243.

Wilson, G.
   1940. Warblers in Mammoth Cave National Park. Ky.
   Warbler 16:40-41.

Wilson Ornithol. Soc.
   1961. Annual report of the conservation committee.
   Wilson Bull. 73(3):310-319.

Wilson Ornithol. Soc.
   1963. Annual report of the conservation committee.
   Wilson Bull. 75(3):295-325.

Wing, L. W.
   1956. Natural history of birds. 539 p. Ronald
   Press, N. Y.

Woodruff, E. S.
   1907. Some interesting records from southern Missouri. Auk 24:348-349

Woodruff, E. S.
   1908. A preliminary list of the birds of Shannon
   and Carter counties, Missouri. Auk 25:191-214.

Worthington, W. W., and W. E. C. Todd
   1926. The birds of the Choctawhatchee Bay region of
   Florida. Wilson Bull. 33:204-229.

Wright, L. M.
    1976.   The interpretation of Bachman's Warbler, an
    endangered species.   Unpublished manuscript.   73
    p.   Clemson Univ. Dep. Recreation and Park Admin.,
    Clemson, S. C.

Zimmer, J. T.
    1926.   Catalog of the Edward E. Ayer Ornithological
    Library, 2 parts.   Field Mus. Nat. Hist. Publ. 239
    and 240, Zool. Ser.   vol. 16, 706 p.   [Although
    this work contains no explicit mention of Bach-
    man's Warbler, it is a voluminous bibliography of
    rare and often well-illustrated works.   Certain
    works listed in it and unavailable to me at this
    writing probably include mention of the species.]

Zimmerman, W.
    1977a. [Painting of Bachman's Warblers.]   Chat
    41(2):front cover.   SEE: Zimmerman 1977b, 1979
    are reprints of this painting.

Zimmerman, W.
    1977b. [Painting of Bachman's Warblers.]   Birding
    9(6):front cover.   SEE: This is a reprint of Zim-
    merman 1977a.

Zimmerman, W.
    1979.   [Bachman's Warbler painting by Wm. Zimmerman.
    No. 1 of ABA's First Print Series.]   Birding
    11:266.   SEE: This is a reprint of Zimmerman
    1977a.

Bachman's Warbler foraging below 1 m in Post Oak seed-
ling, 1958, Charleston Co., S. C.
            Photo courtesy of Walter Dawn.

Listing by Subject

Sequence of subject headings follows that of the *Zoological Record*.

GENERAL:

General Works

Works which are either (1) general works and textbooks; or (2) works containing general information about Bachman's Warblers.

Audubon 1831-1834
Audubon 1841
Baird 1864
Barnes 1954
Berger 1961
Blair et al. 1968
Bond 1956
Buhrman 1977
Chamberlain, E. B. 1958
Chamberlain, E. B. 1974
Chapman 1966
Chapman 1968
Chapman and Reed 1903
Childs 1906
Choate 1973
Clements 1974
Collins 1960
Coues 1869
Deignan 1961
Dingle 1963
Evenden et al. 1977
Faver 1953
Figgins 1945
Fink 1978
Forbush and May 1939
Geffen 1978
Geibel 1875
Griscom 1945
Griscom and Sprunt 1979
Hamel et al. 1982
Hausman 1944

Howell 1928
Imhof 1976
Klimkiewicz and Robbins 1978
LeGrand 1975
Meanley 1951
Oberholser 1938
Reed 1965
Reilly 1954
Richardson 1837
Ridgway 1876
Ridgway 1881b
Robinson and Bolen 1984
Sprunt 1954a
Sprunt and Chamberlain 1970
Stevens 1936
Stevenson 1978
Taylor 1972
USDI Fish & Wildl. Serv. 1978
USDI Fish & Wildl. Serv. Nat. Fish & Wildl. Lab. 1980
USDI Off. Endangered Species and Int. Activ. 1973
Wayne 1906
Wayne 1910a
Zimmer 1926

Field Guides

Bond 1936
Bond 1971
Booth 1962
Bull and Farrand 1977
Farrand 1983
Harrison 1978
Headstrom 1949

Peterson 1947
Peterson 1963
Peterson 1980
Pough 1946
Robbins et al. 1966
Scott 1983
Short 1981

Bibliographies

Harrison 1974
Ridgway 1902

Sharpe 1885
Zimmer 1926

Biographies

Buchheister 1974
Fargo 1934
Griffin 1957
Griscom and Sprunt 1979
Gruson 1972

Northwood 1956
Shuler 1979d
Sprunt 1931
Wright 1976

Illustrations

Audubon 1831-1834
Audubon 1841
Audubon 1966
Baird et al. 1874
Brasher 1962
Buchheister 1974
Bull and Farrand 1977
Chamberlain, E. B. 1958
Chapman 1966
Chapman 1968
Dawn 1958
Dawn 1962
Dick 1956
Dick 1958
Farrand 1983
Forbush and May 1939
Gauthreaux 1976
Gauthreaux 1977
Griscom and Sprunt 1979

Hamel and Gauthreaux 1982
Hirsch 1973
Howell 1932
Imhof 1976
Lowery 1974
Peterson 1947
Peterson 1963
Peterson 1980
Potter et al. 1980
Pough 1946
Robbins 1975
Robbins et al. 1966
Scott 1983
Short 1981
Sprunt 1958
Studer 1888
Zimmerman 1977a
Zimmerman 1977b
Zimmerman 1979

93

Nomenclature

Am. Ornithol. Union 1886
Am. Ornithol. Union 1909
Am. Ornithol. Union 1944a
Audubon 1831-1834
Audubon 1841
Baird 1858
Baird et al. 1874
Coues 1878
Coues 1882

Gundlach 1861a
Hellmayr 1935
Oberholser 1905
Ridgway 1881a
Ridgway 1882
Ridgway 1902
Roads 1912
Sharpe 1885
Swainson 1827

Classification

Am. Ornithol. Union 1886
Am. Ornithol. Union 1957
Am. Ornithol. Union 1983
Audubon 1831-1834
Audubon 1834
Audubon 1839
Audubon 1841
Baird 1858
Baird 1862
Baird et al. 1874
Bonaparte 1838
Bonaparte 1854
Boucard 1876
Coues 1878

Coues 1882
Coues 1903
Gray 1849
Gray 1869
Hamel 1978
Hellmayr 1935
Lowery and Monroe 1968
Maynard 1889-1896
Morony et al. 1975
Ridgway 1881b
Ridgway 1887
Ridgway 1896
Ridgway 1902
Sharpe 1885

Critical Reviews

Amadon 1953
Chapman 1968
Dingle 1963
Evenden et al. 1976a
Evenden et al. 1976b
Evenden et al. 1977
Hamel 1976
Hamel 1977c
Hamel 1979
Hamel and Gauthreaux 1982
Hamel and Hooper 1979a

Hamel and Hooper 1979b
Harrison et al. 1977
Hooper and Hamel 1977
King 1978
Shuler 1976
Shuler 1977g
Sprunt 1954a
Sprunt and Chamberlain
    1970
Stevenson 1972b
Vaughn 1978

Popular Works

Aldrich 1970
Bond 1945a
Brasher 1962
Brooks 1946
Burleigh 1958
Cohen 1976
Cox 1975
Curry-Lindahl 1972
Cutts 1964
Dawn 1962
Fisher et al. 1969
Greenway 1958
Griscom and Sprunt 1979
Grosvenor and Wetmore
    1937
Gruson 1972
Hamel et al. 1976
Harrison 1948
Hausman 1944
Hausman 1946
Howell 1928
Howell 1932
Imhof 1962
Imhof 1976
Laycock 1969
Lowery 1974
McClung 1969

Mackenzie 1977
Meanley 1951
Meanley 1972
Meanley 1975
Murphy and Amadon 1953
New Yorker 1950
Northwood 1956
Oberholser 1938
Oberholser 1974
Odom 1976
Pasquier 1977
Peterson 1948
Potter et al. 1980
Reilly 1968
Robbins 1975
Sprunt 1954a
Sprunt 1954b
Sprunt 1958
Sprunt and Chamberlain
    1970
Stewart 1978
Sutton 1967
Taylor 1972
Trudeau 1981
USDA For. Serv. 1969
Wing 1956

Techniques

Hooper and Hamel 1974

Urbston et al. 1979

MORPHOLOGY

General

Audubon 1834
Averill 1920
Baird 1858
Brewster 1887
Griscom 1923
Hamel 1981

Maynard 1889-1896
Ostroff 1985
Ridgway 1887
Ridgway 1896
Ridgway 1902
Sharpe 1885

Egg

Averill 1924
Harrison 1978
Maynard 1890
Reed 1965

Ridgway 1897
Short 1905
Wayne 1912

Plumage and Plumage Color

Audubon 1834
Audubon 1839
Baird 1858
Blair et al. 1968
Brewster 1891
Brewster 1905
Butler 1900
Coues 1903
Deane 1929
Dingle 1963
Gundlach 1893
Hamel and Gauthreaux 1982
Holmes 1977

Lembeye 1850
Ridgway 1876
Ridgway 1887
Ridgway 1896
Ridgway 1902
Scott 1888a
Sharpe 1885
Shuler 1977c
Stevenson 1938
Wayne 1907a
Wayne 1910a
Widmann 1897

EVOLUTION AND PHYLOGENY

Allen 1893
Hamel 1977c
Mayr and Short 1970

Stein 1968a
Trotter 1887

ECOLOGY

General

Amadon 1953
Coues 1870
Hamel 1977c
Hamel 1980
Hamel 1981
Howell 1928
Imhof 1976

LeGrand and Hamel 1980
Potter et al. 1980
Sprunt and Chamberlain
    1970
Stevenson 1978
Trotter 1887
Widmann 1897

96

Breeding Habitat

Arnow 1908
Barnes 1954
Blake 1948
Brewster 1905
Burleigh 1957
Chamberlain, B. R. 1958
Chamberlain, E. B. 1958
Dawn 1958
Dickson 1978
Dingle 1963
Embody 1907
Evenden et al. 1976a
Evenden et al. 1976b
Evenden et al. 1977
Ficken and Ficken 1968
Gaddy 1979
Hamel 1976
Hamel 1977b
Hamel 1977c
Hamel 1980
Hamel 1981
Hamel and Hooper 1979a
Hamel and Hooper 1979b
Hamel et al. 1977
Hamel et al. 1982
Harrison et al. 1977
Holt 1920
Hooper and Hamel 1977
Howell 1910
Howell 1911
Howell 1928
Howell 1932
Imhof 1962
Imhof 1976
Keeler 1976

King 1978
LeGrand and Hamel 1980
New Yorker 1950
Remsen 1986
Robertson 1962
Short 1905
Shuler 1976
Shuler 1977b
Shuler 1977d
Shuler 1977e
Shuler 1977f
Shuler 1977g
Smith 1915
Sprunt 1954a
Sprunt 1958
Sprunt and Chamberlain 1970
Stevenson 1938
Stevenson 1972b
Stevenson 1975
Stevenson 1978
Tanner 1939
USDI Fish & Wildl. Serv. Nat. Fish & Wildl. Lab. 1980
Urbston et al. 1979
Wayne 1907a
Wayne 1910a
Widmann 1896
Widmann 1897
Widmann 1898
Widmann 1907
Wilson 1918
Woodruff 1907
Woodruff 1908

Territory

Barnes 1954
Dawn 1958

Widmann 1897

Migration

Amadon 1953
Arnow 1908
Averill 1920
Baird 1867
Bond 1956
Bond 1971
Bonhote 1903
Brewster 1891
Brewster and Chapman 1891
Burleigh 1944
Cooke 1904
Cooke 1906
Dingle 1963
Galbraith 1888
Howell 1928
Howell 1932

Imhof 1976
Kopman 1905
Nehrling 1906
Sciple 1950
Scott 1888b
Scott 1890a
Stevenson 1957
Stevenson 1972a
Stevenson 1972b
Stevenson 1975
Wayne 1893
Wayne 1895
Williams 1945
Williams 1950
Worthington and Todd 1926

Winter Habitat

Bond 1957
Bond 1971
Garrido 1985
Gundlach 1865
Gundlach 1876
Gundlach 1893
King 1978

Lembeye 1850
Rappole et al. 1983
Read 1911
Ripley and Moreno 1980
Stevenson 1972b
Terborgh 1974
Terborgh 1980

Ecological Associates

Arnow 1908
Barnes 1954
Brewster 1891
Burleigh 1944
Dawn 1958
Embody 1907
Garrido 1985
Hamel 1977b

Hamel 1981
Horlbeck 1958
Scott 1888b
Scott 1890b
Sprunt 1954b
Stevenson 1938
Wayne 1907a
Widmann 1897

Competition

Barnes 1954
Dawn 1958

Scott 1890a

REPRODUCTION

Breeding Habits

Brewster 1905
Dingle 1963
Howell 1928

Imhof 1976
Wayne 1910a
Widmann 1897

Clutch and Brood Size

Arnow 1908
Bailey 1883
Davie 1898
Dingle 1963
Embody 1907
Hamel 1977d
Holt 1920
Howell 1928
Imhof 1962
Ridgway 1897
Short 1905

Shuler 1979a
Shuler 1979c
Stevenson 1938
Wayne 1907a
Wayne 1907b
Wayne 1910a
Wayne 1910b
Wayne 1918
Widmann 1897
Widmann 1898

Parental Care

Brewster 1905
Stevenson 1938
Verner and Willson 1969

Wayne 1905
Wayne 1907a
Widmann 1897

Size

Bailey 1933
Brewster 1891
Brewster and Chapman 1891
Embody 1907
Evenden et al. 1977
Galbraith 1888
Howell 1910
King 1978
Nehrling 1906

Peterson 1948
Pettingill 1970
Scott 1888b
Sprunt 1954a
Stevenson 1972b
Stevenson 1975
Wayne 1910a
Widmann 1897
Widmann 1898

Endangeredness

Am. Ornithol. Union 1963
Am. Ornithol. Union 1975
Am. Ornithol. Union 1978
Burleigh 1958
Carolina Bird Club 1963
Cox 1975
Culler 1971
Curry-Lindahl 1972
Drury 1974
Evenden et al. 1977
Fisher 1960
Gaddy 1979
Goodwin 1974
Greenway 1958
Griscom 1948
Hamel 1979
Hamel and Hooper 1979a
Hamel and Hooper 1979b
Hooper and Hamel 1979
Keeler 1976
King 1978
Laycock 1969
Lowery 1974
Mackenzie 1977
Meanley 1971
Meanley 1972
Oberholser 1974
Odom 1976
Pasquier 1977
Peterson 1948

Potter et al. 1980
Rappole et al. 1983
Remsen 1986
Shugart et al. 1978
Shuler 1977d
Shuler 1978
Stevenson 1972b
Stevenson 1975
Stevenson 1978
Stevenson 1982
Terborgh 1974
Trotter 1887
USDI Fish & Wildl. Serv.
    1980
USDI Fish & Wildl. Serv.
    Nat. Fish & Wildl.
    Lab. 1980
USDI Off. Endangered
    Species and Int.
    Activ. 1973
Vaughn 1978
Vincent 1966
Wallace and Mahan 1975
Wilcove and Terborgh 1984
Wilson Ornithol. Soc.
    1961
Wilson Ornithol. Soc.
    1963
Wright 1976

Protection

Am. Ornithol. Union 1944b
Am. Ornithol. Union 1978
Black 1979
Campbell 1977
Chamberlain 1974
Evenden et al. 1976a
Evenden et al. 1976b
Evenden et al. 1977
Hamel 1980

King 1978
Natl. Wildl. Fed. 1976
Olendorff and Zeedyk 1978
USDA For. Serv. 1977
USDI Off. Endangered
  Species and Int.
  Activ. 1973
Vaughn 1978

Searches

Brewster 1886
Curtis 1978
Evenden et al. 1977
Florida Game and Freshwater
  Fish Comm. 1976
Galbraith 1888
Ganier 1916
Hamel 1976
Hamel 1977a
Hamel 1977b
Hamel 1979
Hamel and Hooper 1979a
Hamel and Hooper 1979b

Hamel et al. 1976
Hooper and Hamel 1974
Imhof 1977
LeGrand 1979
Lowery 1974
Meanley 1972
Mengel 1965
Peterson 1948
Ridgway 1878
Stevenson 1972b
Stevenson 1975
Wilson 1940
Wright 1976

BEHAVIOR

General

Audubon 1834
Barnes 1954
Brewster 1891
Brewster 1905
Burleigh 1957
Chamberlain, E. B. 1958
Clark 1938
Dawn 1958
Dawn 1962
Dingle 1963
Gilbert 1983
Hanes 1958
Horlbeck 1958

Howell 1928
Meanley 1972
Meanley and Mitchell 1958
New Yorker 1950
Scott 1890a
Shuler 1977b
Shuler 1977e
Wayne 1901
Wayne 1895
Wayne 1907a
Widmann 1897
Woodruff 1908

Vocalization

Barnes 1954
Bondeson 1977
Brewster 1891
Burleigh 1958
Chamberlain, E. B. 1958
Dingle 1963
Griscom and Sprunt 1979
Hanes 1958
Howell 1928
Imhof 1976
Jones 1900
Newman 1954
New Yorker 1950
Saunders 1951
Scott 1890a

Shuler 1977c
Smith 1915
Sprunt and Chamberlain 1970
Stein 1968a
Stein 1968b
Stevenson 1938
Stevenson 1972a
Stevenson 1975
Thayer 1906
Wayne 1907b
Wayne 1910a
Widmann 1897
Woodruff 1908

Foraging and Feeding

Arnow 1908
Balboa 1941
Barnes 1954
Bond 1957
Brewster 1891
Dawn 1958
Embody 1907
Faaborg and Terborgh 1980
Ficken and Ficken 1968
Gundlach 1876
Gundlach 1893
Hamel 1981

Howell 1928
Imhof 1962
Lembeye 1850
Meanley and Mitchell 1958
Scott 1888b
Scott 1890a
Shuler 1977b
Shuler 1977e
Studer 1888
Widmann 1897
Woodruff 1908

DISEASES

Sciple 1950

Bahamas

Bond 1956
Bond 1971
Bonhote 1903
Brudenell-Bruce 1975

Cooke 1905
King 1978
Paterson 1972
Riley 1905

Cuba

Am. Ornithol. Union 1957
Am. Ornithol. Union 1983
Baird 1867
Balboa 1941
Barbour 1923
Barbour 1943
Bond 1957
Brewer 1860
Cooke 1904
Cooke 1905
Cory 1885
Cory 1886
Cory 1889
Cory 1892
Dingle 1963
Garrido 1985

Garrido and Garcia
    Montana 1975
Gochfeld 1974
Gochfeld 1979
Gruson 1976
Gundlach 1855
Gundlach 1861a
Gundlach 1861b
Gundlach 1865
Gundlach 1876
Gundlach 1893
Keast 1980
King 1978
Lembeye 1850
Ripley and Moreno 1980
Stevenson 1972b

Isle of Pines

Read 1909a
Read 1909b
Read 1911
Read 1913

Reed 1911
Stevenson 1972b
Todd 1916

United States, General

Am. Ornithol. Union 1957
Am. Ornithol. Union 1983
Averill 1920
Barnes 1954
Cooke 1904
Cooke 1905
Dingle 1963
Gauthreaux 1973
Griscom 1951
Griscom 1952
Griscom 1954
Gruson 1976
Hamel 1981
Hamel 1984
Hamel et al. 1982
King 1978
LeGrand and Hamel 1980

Meanley 1951
Meanley 1972
Meanley and Mitchell 1958
Mengel 1964
Pettingill 1951
Robbins 1950
Robbins et al. 1975
Shuler 1977d
Stein 1968a
Stevenson 1972b
Stevenson 1978
Studer 1888
Tucker 1979
USDI Fish & Wildl. Serv.
    Nat. Fish & Wildl.
    Lab. 1980

U. S., Alabama

Golsan and Holt 1914
Holt 1920
Howell 1928
Imhof 1962
Imhof 1966
Imhof 1976
Keeler 1976

Newman 1955
Newman 1958
Newman and Warter 1959b
Saunders 1908
Stevenson 1938
Stevenson 1972b

U. S., Arkansas

Baerg 1951
Howell 1911
Imhof 1977
James and Neal 1987
Riley and Riley 1979

Smith 1915
Wheeler 1924
Widmann 1896
Widmann 1897

U. S., Florida

Bailey 1925
Barber 1985
Baynard 1942
Bond 1956
Brewster 1891
Butler 1934
Chapman 1889
Howell 1932
Lane 1981
Merriam 1887
Nehrling 1906
Newman and Warter 1959a
Rehn 1905
Scott 1887
Scott 1888a
Scott 1888b
Scott 1890a
Scott 1890b
Scott 1892
Sprunt 1954a
Sprunt 1963
Stevenson 1956
Stevenson 1958
Stevenson 1975
Stevenson 1976
Stevenson 1978
Wayne 1893
Wayne 1895
Wayne 1907a
Weston 1965
Williams 1904
Williams 1907
Worthington and Todd 1926

U. S., Georgia

Arnow 1908
Bassett 1941
Burleigh 1958
Denton and Hopkins 1969
Denton et al. 1977
Greene 1933
Greene et al. 1945
Hoxie 1911
Johnson and Landers 1982
LaPrade 1922
USDI Fish and
    Wildl. Serv. 1971
Wayne 1912
Wayne 1925

U. S., Illinois

Bohlen 1978
Brewer 1958
Fawks 1936
Gault 1922
George 1971
Graber et al. 1983
Kleen and Bush 1971
Mayfield 1950
Ridgway 1874
Ridgway 1878
Ridgway 1881c
Ridgway 1889
Smith 1941
Smith and Parmalee 1955

U. S., Indiana

Butler 1900
Keller et al. 1979
Mumford and Keller 1975
Wilson 1918

U. S., Kentucky

Bailey 1933
Barbour et al. 1973
Burns 1908
Embody 1907
Figgins 1945
Funkhouser 1925

Mengel 1948
Mengel 1965
Pindar 1923
Wilson 1922
Wilson 1940

U. S., Louisiana

Allen 1888
Allison 1904
Beyer 1900
Galbraith 1888
Gee 1977
Imhof 1973
Imhof 1977
Kopman 1905
Kopman 1915

Lawrence 1887a
Lawrence 1887b
Lowery 1974
Lowery and Newman 1952
Newman 1954
Oberholser 1938
Stevenson 1975
Tanner 1939

U. S., Mississippi

Burleigh 1944
Burleigh 1957

Kopman 1915
Sciple 1950

U. S., Missouri

Blake 1948
Cunningham 1940
Griscom 1948
Howell 1910
Howell 1911
Imhof 1977
Korte and Fredrickson

1977
Short 1905
Widmann 1897
Widmann 1898
Widmann 1907
Woodruff 1907
Woodruff 1908

U. S., North Carolina

Brimley 1891
Brimley 1917
Brimley 1930
Cooper et al. 1977
Hader 1969

LeGrand 1975
Parnell et al. 1978
Pearson et al. 1942
Potter et al. 1980

U. S., Oklahoma

Baumgartner 1960   Sutton 1967
Baumgartner 1963

U. S., South Carolina

Am. Ornithol. Union 1975   Johnston 1962
Bass 1979a   LeGrand 1979
Bass 1979b   Lesser Squawk 1958a
Black 1979   Lesser Squawk 1958b
Bull 1958   Lesser Squawk 1958c
Burton 1970   Lesser Squawk 1959
Carolina Bird Club 1950   Lesser Squawk 1960
Chamberlain, B. R. 1958   Lesser Squawk 1961a
Chamberlain, B. R. 1959   Lesser Squawk 1961b
Chamberlain 1960a   Lesser Squawk 1962
Chamberlain 1960b   Lesser Squawk 1969
Chamberlain 1961a   Lesser Squawk 1973
Chamberlain 1961b   Nugent 1976
Chamberlain 1961c   Potter et al. 1980
Chamberlain 1962   Rea 1909
Chamberlain 1968   Rea and Weston 1909
Chamberlain 1978   Shuler 1976
Chamberlain, E. B. 1958   Shuler 1977a
Chamberlain, E. B. 1959   Shuler 1977b
Chamberlain and   Shuler 1977c
   Chamberlain 1948   Shuler 1977d
Coleman 1961a   Shuler 1977e
Coleman 1961b   Shuler 1979b
Deane 1929   Shuler and Sanders 1977
Denton and Chamberlain   Shuler et al. 1978
   1950   Shuler et al. 1979
Evenden et al. 1977   Sprunt 1954b
Forsythe 1978   Sprunt 1958
Gibbes 1848   Sprunt 1965
Griscom 1948   Sprunt and Chamberlain
Griscom and Sprunt 1979   1970
Hamel 1976   Stansell 1976
Hamel 1977a   Teulings 1978
Hamel 1977b   True 1883
Hamel and Hooper 1979a   USDA For. Serv. Southern
Hamel and Hooper 1979b   Region 1985a
Hamel et al. 1976   USDA For. Serv. Southern
Holmes 1977   Region 1985b
Horlbeck 1958   USDI Fish & Wildl. Serv.
Howe 1978   1967

U. S., South Carolina, cont.

Urbston et al. 1979   Wayne 1910a
Wayne 1901   Wayne 1917
Wayne 1905   Wayne 1918
Wayne 1907a   Wright 1976
Wayne 1907b

U. S., Tennessee

Eagar and Hatcher 1982   Ganier 1917
Ganier 1916   Ganier 1933

U. S., Texas

Baumgartner 1951   Oberholser 1974
Gunter 1972   Peterson 1963

U. S., Virginia

Bailey 1913   Murray 1933
Barnes 1954   Murray 1952
Clark 1938   Palmer 1894
Geffen 1978   Potter and Murray 1954
Larner et al. 1979   Ruch 1954
Meanley 1951

Bachman's Warbler on a branch of water oak, anodized
aluminum sculpture (Hirsch 1973).

Photo by Willard Hirsch.

About the Author

Paul B. Hamel currently holds the title of Zoologist in the Ecological Services Division of the Tennessee Department of Conservation, where he conducts inventory and research studies on endangered and threatened species and their Tennessee habitats.